YUAN MEI

Translated by Arthur Waley

THE NINE SONGS
THE REAL TRIPITAKA
THE POETRY AND CAREER OF LI PO
THE LIFE AND TIMES OF PO CHÜ-I
CHINESE POEMS
MONKEY
THREE WAYS OF THOUGHT IN ANCIENT CHINA
THE ANALECTS OF CONFUCIUS
THE BOOK OF SONGS
THE WAY AND ITS POWER
THE TALE OF GENJI
THE NŌ PLAYS OF JAPAN
THE TEMPLE AND OTHER POEMS
MORE TRANSLATIONS FROM THE CHINESE
THE PILLOW-BOOK OF SEI SHŌNAGON

Yuan Mei at Fifty

ARTHUR WALEY

YUAN MEI

Eighteenth Century Chinese Poet

Il est probable qu'il n'y a rien de plus sain pour un homme, comme pour tout animal, que de suivre ses goûts.

Remi de Gourmont

STANFORD UNIVERSITY PRESS
STANFORD, CALIFORNIA

TO

OSBERT SITWELL

Stanford University Press
Stanford, California
Originating publisher: George Allen & Unwin Ltd, London
First published in the United States by
The Macmillan Company, 1957
Reissued by Stanford University Press in 1970
Printed in the United States of America
Cloth SBN 8047-0718-9
Paper SBN 8047-0719-7
LC 70-107646

PREFACE

THIS book is meant chiefly for the general reader with no knowledge of pre-Soviet China. I have assumed that he will not have heard of any of the people mentioned, except possibly the Emperor Ch'ien Lung, and I have explained, either in the text or in the glossary, all specifically Chinese terms and allusions. Chinese names, for those unfamiliar with the language, are hard to remember and I have tried, on principles explained below (p. 213), to reduce to a minimum the number of persons mentioned. When possible I have given the dates of people who figure in the story, partly to indicate whether they were contemporaries or belong to past history, and partly because it may be inferred, if the dates are known, that they were people of some reputation and importance.

I have not attempted to put down seriatim everything that happened to Yuan Mei or to discuss everything that he wrote. There is still scope for a full-scale biography, addressed to specialists, and dealing with every aspect of his life and writings. I have concentrated rather on whatever in his story has a general human interest, and on translating such of his poems as can be made intelligible without an undue amount of explanation.

Personally, I find him a lovable, witty, generous, affectionate, hot-tempered, wildly prejudiced man; a writer of poetry that even at its lightest always has an undertone of deep feeling and at its saddest may at any moment light a sudden spark of fun. My hope is that this book will make a certain number of readers feel about him as I do.

CONTENTS

PROVINCES of CHINA
IN THE
18TH. CENTURY
0
300 Miles
Peking
CHIHLI
SHANSI
SHANTUNG
KOREA
KANSU
SHENSI
HONAN
KIANGNAN
Nanking
Hangchow
HUPEH
SZECHWAN
CHEKIANG
KIANGSI
HUNAN
FUKHIEN
KWEICHOW
YUNNAN
KWANGSI
KWANGTUNG
Canton

CHAPTER ONE

At Hangchow

YUAN MEI was born at Hangchow in 1716. The family was poor and his father Yuan Pin (1678–1752) was obliged to accept humble secretarial posts in a succession of different provinces. He was looked after chiefly by a widowed aunt who lived with them. About his mother we hear very little. It was his Aunt Shen who 'when I was cold, wrapped me up, scratched my back when it itched, washed my face in the morning and gave me my bath at night'. When his hair was cut he cried unless some grown-up person told him stories. His aunt had collected a great repertory of stories such as a child of four or five could understand, gathered from the standard histories and from books of anecdotes. 'Thus before I went to school', he says, 'the names of all the great figures of Han, Chin, T'ang and Sung times were already thoroughly familiar to me.' A little later when he began trying to read the Classic of History (*Shu Ching*) and was frowning over the strange archaic words which he did not know how to pronounce, Aunt Shen would slip up to his side and pressing close to him 'like a sword at the hip' would help him with whispered promptings.

When he was six he began to have formal lessons with a Mr. Shih Chung, whom he discovered to be a poet. He got hold secretly of his tutor's copy of the T'ang History and found written in it a poem which he greatly admired:

It is not true that Huai-en betrayed his prince's favour;
Historians have failed to right the wrong done to his name.
Far away at Ling-chou, amid the wild steppes
Until now night by night a hero's ghost weeps.

P'u-ku Huai-en was a T'ang general who, after rendering conspicuous services to the dynasty, was accused in 765 of plotting with the Uighurs and Tibetans to overthrow the regime. He died suddenly, before he had time to exculpate himself. Yuan Mei copied out the poem; and this was the beginning of his life-long habit of noting down verses that he admired. But his first general introduction to poetry happened two years later: 'One day my tutor's friend Chang Tzu-nan came to the school-room with a book that he wanted to sell. As my tutor, Mr. Shih, was out, he left a note for him in which he said, "I happen at the moment to be very hard pressed. I have brought a copy of the 'Choice of Old Poems' in four volumes, and if you could let me have two ounces of silver for it you would really be saving my life, and I should be inexpressibly grateful".'

Here it should be said that the book referred to (the *Ku Shih Hsuan*) was an anthology of poetry from the earliest times down to about 1400 made by the great critic Wang Shih-chen (1634–1711) and first printed in 1697. 'My mother's brother', Yuan Mei continues, 'saw the note and said to my mother, "If Mr. Chang makes such a piteous appeal for a mere matter of two ounces of silver, he ought certainly to have them, whether we keep the book or not." . . . When my tutor was out and during the holidays at the turn of the year I used not only to read and recite them, from the Nineteen Old Poems of the Han dynasty down to the time of Li Po and Tu Fu, but also made imitations of them. That was how my study of poetry began. How much I owe to Mr. Chang's impecuniosity!' Mr. Chang was presumably too proud to take the book away.

Yuan Mei could only read poetry surreptitiously because he was now studying for the First Degree in which he would be tested principally in knowledge of the Confucian 'Four Books', and time spent on reading for pleasure was regarded by his tutor as wasted.

At the age of eleven, in 1727, he passed the Boys' Test, which enabled him to sit for the First Degree, which he took five or six years earlier than was usual. He was now an accredited National Student, entitled to wear on his cap the silver badge which had been accorded to students by the Emperor the year before. But in other ways he was still a child. His tutor took him to the college, and at night (being frightened to sleep on a bed alone) he was allowed to go on sleeping on his grandmother's lap. At this period he began to have a passion for books: 'Books', he wrote long afterwards, 'became to me dearer than life itself. Each time I came to a book-shop, my feet remained rooted to the spot. I had no money to buy books with, but I used to dream that I had bought them and had them at home with me.' (See below, p. 191.)

One of the earliest pieces which he thought worth preserving was an essay on Kuo Chü, one of the Twenty-four Paragons of Filial Piety. Kuo Chü said one day to his wife, 'We are so poor that my mother is not getting enough to eat. Let us get rid of our little boy who has such a big appetite. I can have other sons; but I can never have another mother.' They decided to dig a hole and bury the child alive. They had dug only three feet when, as a reward for Kuo's filial piety, they found a golden pot, inscribed with the words: 'Heaven's gift to Kuo Chü.' This story horrified Aunt Shen, who wrote the poem:

It is all wrong to quote Kuo as an example of Filial Piety.
How can he have thought that such a sacrifice would give his mother pleasure?
Surely after seeing a pretty child wantonly done to death
The sight of food would only have hurt the old grandmother's feelings. . . .

Under his aunt's instruction Yuan Mei wrote a little essay on the subject in which he said: 'If he could not rear him, why have a son? Having a son, how could he bear to slay him? Fancy burying the son because he took away what the mother might have been eating! To kill one whom one loves merely for the sake of food is to treat him as though he were an animal', and so on. He was evidently pleased with this composition, for not long afterwards he showed it to the Principal of the Wan-sung Academy, where he was studying. The Principal (Yang Sheng-wu, *c.* 1680–1754) returned it with the comment (scribbled in at the end of the essay): 'Your prose, like the armies of General Hsiang Yü, leaves utter annihilation behind it wherever you pass. For one who is still a mere boy, your methods are indeed heroic.' There may have been a slight irony in the comment, but Yuan Mei did not take it in that sense, and felt greatly encouraged.

In 1734 an immensely learned man named Shuai Nien-tsu, who was one of the compilers of the Comprehensive Geography of the Empire (*Ta-Ch'ing I-t'ung Chih*), arrived as Commissioner of Education at Hangchow. On his rounds of inspection he came to Yuan Mei's academy and asked him, among other questions, if he could explain the expressions 'national horse' and 'public horse' (*kuo-ma* and *kung-ma*). 'I replied', writes Yuan Mei, ' "These expressions occur in the 'Sayings of the Feudal States' (*Kuo Yü*), with commentary by Wei Chao. But what they mean I really do not know." '

There was indeed a trap here, because *kuo-ma*, which in Yuan Mei's day meant 'national horse', in feudal times meant a horse belonging to the common people of the country, as opposed to horses belonging to the feudal ruler. But the Commissioner let him down easily. 'At your age', he said, 'it is quite enough that you should know where the expressions come from. You can't be expected to explain them.' 'Reading without understanding' was indeed a perfectly legitimate practice, hallowed long ago by the famous ancient poet T'ao Ch'ien who when he read books 'Did not try very much to understand; but whenever he came across some sentiment that was congenial to him was in such ecstasy that he forgot to go to his meals.' On the other hand, not to know in what book an expression occurred was considered unforgivably boorish.

In 1736 a special examination (the *Po-hsüeh Hung-tz'u*), of a kind that occurred only at long intervals, was to be held at Peking. Its object was to select men of very high literary attainments, who could be employed in writing official histories and the like. The year before, a test was held at Hangchow, in order to discover suitable local candidates for the Peking examination. We know very little about what happened at this test, except that on the day when it took place it was snowing, and the test-poem was to be entitled *Spring Snow*, and was to consist of twenty-four lines. Yuan Mei went in for the test and came out 'in the vanguard'. The Peking examination was not to be held till the late autumn of 1736 and Yuan Mei now set out to visit his uncle, Yuan Hung, who was working in the office of the Governor of Kwangsi province, at Kuei-lin. It seems probable that this was not a mere pleasure-trip or the fulfilment of a family duty, but was connected rather with family business of some kind. Remittances from Yuan Mei's father arrived very irregularly, and he was perhaps charged to discover whether the uncle could not do something towards supporting the family at Hangchow. The expenses of the journey were partly paid for by a prominent citizen of Hangchow, a Mr. Ch'ai. 'When I was young', Yuan Mei writes, 'I was high-spirited and rather wild and flighty in my behaviour. Most of the elderly Hangchow notabilities tended to disapprove of me, but Ch'ai Chih-yuan took to me from the first.' It happened that Ch'ai's brother was going to take up a post as tutor in a family at Kao-an, about half-way to Kuei-lin. He took Yuan Mei with him as his guest, and lent him twelve ounces of silver (about £4 at the then rate of exchange), but it proved an inadequate provision and, 'sprawling on a wretched punt-boat I suffered the last extremities of hunger and cold'. About the uncle we know little except one charming anecdote: 'When he was young my uncle went to visit some relatives at Chen-chiang, and lodged in the house of a certain blacksmith. The blacksmith's wife turned out to be an educated woman and my uncle and she started a correspondence in verse, which for some time went on very happily, without leading to any impropriety. On one occasion he tried to go further, but she pulled him up, saying, "I am the daughter of a Bachelor of Arts and since my childhood I have had a passion for literature. But after my father's death my people were tricked by a match-maker into marrying me to someone who turned out to be an artisan, completely devoid of education. So he blows his bellows, while I write my poems, which is depressing. If through my friendship with you a few of my poor verses become known to people in good positions, then I shall be contented. But all other demonstrations of feeling I can only accept if they stop short at the limit imposed by the rules of propriety." He tried again several times; but she went no further than to promise him with tears in her eyes that in some future incarnation she would be his. My uncle respected her for her fidelity to the blacksmith and did not try to force her.'

Two years later he came to Chen-chiang again. The smithy had been abandoned and no one knew what had become of the blacksmith and his wife. Twelve years later in Kuei-lin he met another blacksmith. This man too could not read or write; but he made poems, which he got other people to write down for him. My uncle used often to say to me, 'If only it had been this blacksmith that my friend had married, what a happy pair they would have made'.

Yuan Mei's *Collected Poems*, which are arranged chronologically, begin in this year; his earlier poems (except for a few afterwards inserted in a supplement) he did not think worth preserving. One of the poems written on the way to Kuei-lin, records a visit to a village school near P'ing-hsiang, now a thickly populated industrial area, but then a remote and unsophisticated spot:

I saw in the distance peach-orchards in leaf,
But did not know what village it was.
I stopped the boat, tucked up my coat-tails and walked
Attracted by hearing the sound of a book being read.
At a wicker gate school-children were gathered,
Sitting in rows, decent and orderly.
When they heard that I had come from Hangchow
A look of delight stirred in every face.
They all came to me, bringing their lesson-books,
Wanting to hear something they had never heard.
Seeing they wished it I explained a few passages
While they sat in a circle, constantly nodding their heads.
When I turned to leave, they brought me chicken and millet
And lifted for me the earthen jar of wine.
Shouldering their hoes, fathers and elder brothers
Back from the fields also came to peep.
They begged their honoured guest not to hurry,
They took no thought that dusk was closing fast.
I told them I was travelling on a special errand,
Was a craft that could not anchor while the wind blew.
When they heard that I was not in a position to stay
Those good people filled their handkerchiefs with tears.
Clutching my coat they brought me aboard my ship,
One after another telling me their names.
'Who knows', they said, 'when we shall meet again!'
'Take care of yourself on the journey to come.'
I was touched by their simple, unspoiled kindness;
It was like meeting peasants of a pristine reign.
I knew now that a 'Peach Blossom Valley'
Is still to be found somewhere in the world of men.
My one regret is that I must leave it;
I turn my head; there are only white clouds.

The legend of the Peach-blossom Valley tells how a traveller came to a remote spot where the inhabitants had for centuries been cut off from all contact with the outside world and still lived in the happy simplicity of primeval ages.

At Kuei-lin his uncle met him with the depressing words: 'You ought not to have come.' But the uncle's employer, Chin Hung (1678–1740), at once took a fancy to him and sent to Court a special recommendation in which he said: 'I have had ample opportunities of studying his character. He is of a quiet and peaceable disposition, his conduct is orderly and circumspect. At a time when the Empire is looking for fresh talent, here is just the material that is required.' 'Whenever the Governor was interviewing his subordinates,' writes Yuan Mei, 'after business was over he used often to quote some line or whole poem of mine, reciting it with great relish, and mention some instance of my good manners or behaviour. Having once accidentally heard him doing this, from behind a screen, I fell into the habit of always eavesdropping when he had visitors. There was a verse in one of the poems I addressed to him in which I said:

To the Palace a thousand miles away you addressed a laudatory statement;
When seated with your band of officials you extolled my compositions.

And this was indeed a plain statement of fact.'

When he left, the Governor not only gave him 120 ounces of silver, but sent a servant with him to look after him on the journey.

CHAPTER TWO

At Peking

AT the special examination there were nearly two hundred candidates, of whom Yuan Mei was the youngest, while the oldest was Wan Ching (1659–1741), descendant of a long line of famous scholars and son of one of the eight brothers who were known as the Eight Dragons of the Wan Family. Long ago Wan Ching, now seventy-five, had been one of the compilers of the *K'ang Hsi Tz'u Tien*, the most famous of all Chinese dictionaries. Yuan Mei's extreme youth caused a great sensation, and many people of consequence called at his lodgings simply out of curiosity, determined to find out for themselves whether it was really true that he was only twenty. The special examination involved writing essays on politico-ethical themes, and a poem of fixed length and metre, the even lines of which all had to rhyme with a given syllable. The subject of the poem was 'The Golden Pheasant dancing before the Mirror', twenty-four lines and seven syllables to the line, rhyming with *shan* throughout. The first necessity, of course, was to know the story to which the title alluded. Once upon a time the people of a distant province sent as tribute to the Capital a golden pheasant. When it saw itself in the huge bronze mirror that stood outside the palace gates, it began to dance, and danced on and on till it died. It is a fine subject for a poem; but evidently Yuan Mei was not satisfied with what he wrote, for he did not include the poem in his collected works.

Neither the oldest nor the youngest candidate was among the fifteen who passed. Yuan Mei was bitterly disappointed, because he had hoped 'to be quit forever of examination essays'. These examination essays (or sermons, as one might call them) had to be composed according to very strict rules. The examiners gave out a text from the Confucian 'Four Books', which the candidate had to expound in an essay of fixed length (generally about six hundred words), dividing his composition into eight parts—exordium, expansion of exordium, opening of exposition and so on, down to 'Grand Conclusion'. These 'eight-legged' sermons had long ago been denounced by the great scholar Ku Yen-wu (1613–1682), who maintained that the insistence upon them in public examinations had done more harm to Chinese culture than the Burning of the Books. Yuan Mei, who detested rigid forms of all kinds, had a great natural aversion to eight-legged essays and had never taken the trouble to perfect himself in them. But he saw now that his only chance of obtaining a post lay in passing the ordinary Second and Third Degree examinations. For the next two years he worked furiously at 'eight-legs', almost abandoning general study and reading, and did indeed become a master in this rather ignoble art. A collection of model examination-essays by him, *Yuan T'ai-shih Kao* (Academician Yuan's Drafts), became a standard textbook for candidates, and through it his name became known to many people who scarcely knew of him as a poet.

The candidates for the special examination were given an allowance that was supposed to keep them for a month. Yuan Mei was soon in great straits.

'There were hurricanes of wind; first it rained and then it snowed, and I had nothing to wear but an unlined silk coat.' He called one day upon T'ang Shou-tsu, Vice-President of the Court of Sacrificial Worship (1690–1759). 'We had a talk, and it seems that he was much struck by me, for next day he sent Chu P'ei-lien, now an Academician, to tell me that he (T'ang) would like to give me one of his daughters in marriage.' Yuan Mei was obliged to refuse the offer, as he was already affianced to the child of a Mr. Wang of Hangchow. 'But he continued to show the utmost sympathy for me. Whenever I came to see him, he always gave me something to eat, and he would lay a hand on my back and say "Are you sure you are warm enough?". Later on, when the hot weather came, he always asked me to take a bath. He would come and put a finger into the tub and say, "It's not hot enough yet; you had better wait a little." '

Yuan Mei wrote an enormous number of biographical epitaphs, and he has often been rightly accused of great inaccuracy as regards small details of fact. Indeed, the value of these epitaphs is not as history, but (at any rate when he was writing about friends) as vivid documents of feeling. It was in evocatory human touches, such as the finger in the bath-tub, that he excels.

He succeeded in getting a place as tutor in the family of a Mr. Wang Wan. But after a short time Mr. Wang went off to a post in the provinces and took his family with him. 'I was left entirely in the lurch', says Yuan Mei, 'and had no idea what was going to become of me. However, a certain Secretary to the Cabinet called Chao, who had also been living with Mr. Wang, comforted me by saying, "Don't you worry! Although Wang has gone, I have hired his house, and his kitchen will still be working." After that, awake or asleep, we spent all our time together, constantly showing each other our compositions and exchanging corrections and criticisms. After some while I was engaged as tutor to the family of the present head of the Board of Rites, Lord Chi, and parted from Secretary Chao. At that time, had it not been for Lord Chi, Secretary Chao would have had to go on feeding me indefinitely, and had it not been for the secretary's generosity, I could not have held out till Lord Chi sent for me.' 'Lord Chi', it should be explained, was Chi Huang (1711–1794), celebrated both as an authority on river conservancy and as a calligrapher. Yuan Mei owed his introduction to his place in the Chi family to another Mr. Chao

(Chao Ta-ch'ing, 1686–1749). 'I waited upon him with some of my writings in my sleeve. He was much struck by them, and I asked him if he could not get me an "eating place" (i.e. a family where he would get board and lodging in return for teaching the children). He went out there and then to see about it, and that same evening I got my invitation from Lord Chi.' Despite his material difficulties and the fact that a large part of his time was taken up by tutoring and working to improve himself in the hated 'examination-essay' style, he made an immense number of friends, becoming a sort of ringleader among the poets and scholars whom the special examination had drawn to the Capital. The only one of these friends from whom he felt he could learn anything and to whom he looked up as a master was Hu T'ien-yu (1696–1758), a proud and erratic scholar who was pursued by consistent ill-fortune. His father died just at the wrong moment, and being in mourning Hu T'ien-yu could not take part in the special examination, to which he had been summoned owing to a particular recommendation by the President of the Board of Rites. He was allowed by special privilege to attend a supplementary examination next year; but in the middle of it he was seized with a violent fit of nose-bleeding and had to give up. Crowded audiences used at this time to assemble and watch him dash off compositions on any theme suggested, a thousand words at a time, his brush flying over the paper as though bewitched. He was too proud to court the great (a very necessary thing to do in the eighteenth century, not only in China, if one wanted to get on in the world), and apparently even too proud to accept jobs when they were offered to him. The great Manchu minister Ortai, of whom we shall hear more later, admired Hu T'ien-yu's writings and suggested that he might be used in the revision of the 'Comprehensive Geography'. But someone who knew him better said, 'Hu is an extraordinary fellow. The one way to ensure that he does not come is to send for him'; and the suggestion was dropped. His writings, once celebrated, are today almost forgotten, there being (except perhaps in Formosa) very few people who want to read eighteenth-century imitations of ninth-century prose. The first time Yuan Mei met him Hu said, 'There are plenty of people who have a pretty talent, but very few who have extraordinary talent. I consider you to be one of those who have extraordinary talent. If while you are still young you work hard to nourish it, we shall see in you, Sir, the prose of the T'ang dynasty live again.' Fortunately, Yuan Mei, though no doubt greatly flattered at the time, did not nourish his talent in this particular way, and his prose style of later years, charming and unique, was anything but a re-hash.

In the autumn of 1738 he at last succeeded in obtaining his Second Degree. He had to write an essay on the text 'scrupulous in his own conduct and lenient only in his dealings with the people', from the sixth book of the *Analects*. Yuan Mei wrote, 'If he applies to his dealings with the people the same principles that he is true to at home, then his lenience will spring from scruple. Scruple is the basis of government, not something arrived at by practising lenience to others. If it exists in his dealings with himself, it will manifest itself in lenience to others, which can spring only from severity towards oneself.' The examiner, Teng Shih-min (1712–1775), wrote in the margin: 'Shows complete grasp of the essence of government. Reads like a Memorial drawn up by some prominent statesman.' Yuan Mei continued till the end of his life to feel deep gratitude to this appreciative examiner. Teng, after a brilliant start to his career, retired at an early age to his home in Szechwan, where he spent almost all the rest of his life. It may have been partly his example that encouraged Yuan Mei, ten years later, to adopt a similar course. In 1768 he addressed to his revered examiner a poem in which he says:

What agony it was thirty years ago
At Peking, waiting for the lists to appear!
I was staying for the night at Mr. Ni's house,

And was hurrying home, prancing along through the dark.
On the way I met someone who told me I had passed;
I was bowled over by this thunderclap of joy and surprise.
I thought it was a mistake, thought it was only a dream;
I was in a sorry state of doubt and dread.
Yet it was true; that staunch master Teng,
His two eyes freshened by the autumn light,
Had written that my name was to figure on the list,
Had rescued me out of my dark abyss.
Do not say I had earned it by my literary powers;
When have letters ever had influence?
Do not say that my horoscope was good;
When have horoscopes said the last word?
Parents, however much they love a child,
Have not the power to place him among the chosen few.
Only the examiner can bring the young to notice,
And out of darkness carry them up to Heaven!

In 1739 he got his Third Degree and also passed the Palace Examination and became a scholar in the Han-lin Academy. He was now a servant of the Throne, and in a short poem he records his feelings upon first putting on his official robes:

I have learnt how to get into my Court dress, but it still feels queer;
When the time came I was strangely loath to take off my blue shirt.
I told my servant to fold it nicely and lay it in an empty box.
A time may come when I want to see it, to remind me of old days.

The subject of the poem set in the Palace Examination was the line, 'Borne on the wind, a suggestion of jade bridle-bells'. 'I thought it necessary', writes Yuan Mei, 'to emphasize the idea contained in the word "suggestion", and I wrote in one couplet of my poem:

I suspect that the sound comes from the Forbidden Courtyards
Whose inhabitants are far off as the Milky Way.

'The examiners, as I afterwards learnt, were of the opinion that the language of the lines was not sufficiently ornate, and intended to plough me. But the President of the Board of Punishments, Yin-chi-shan, was of a different mind. "This fellow uses his wits", he said, "and is certainly a young man of talent. The only trouble is that he has not yet mastered the particular style that has to be adopted in writing at Imperial Command. But after all, it is precisely in order to teach them this style that scholars are trained at the Han-lin. If the Emperor raises any objection when the papers are laid before him, I undertake to put matters right." '

This was the beginning of Yuan Mei's relationship with the old Manchu statesman who soon became not only his most influential patron, but also one of his staunchest friends. Yin-chi-shan (1696–1771) belonged to the Janggiya Clan of Manchus who had settled on the Chinese border long before the Manchu conquest of China and had consequently become early tinged with Chinese culture. During his long life he held a succession of the highest official posts in which he became famous for his fair-dealing and easiness of approach. He was devoted to literature or perhaps, as one might more truly say, to literary games. He had a passion for those ingenious interchanges in which poems have to be written using the same rhymes as those used by the 'player' who leads off. Yuan Mei detested this game and it was only to humour this great man, to whom he felt endless gratitude and affection, that he sometimes consented to take a hand in it.

His other great Manchu supporter was Ortai (1680–1745), whom I have already mentioned. Ortai was an able administrator and also a great patron of literature. A few years ago

Ch'ien Lung (the only Chinese Emperor whose name is a household word in the West) had ascended the throne at the age of twenty-four, and was for some time entirely guided by the experienced statesmen whom his father had trusted. Foremost of these was Ortai, who was for some time the virtual ruler of China.

After the examination for the Third Degree Ortai said to one of the examiners, Chiang P'u (1708–1761), 'Really, this year's candidates are enough to make one die of shame. I looked through the papers, and in my opinion none of them were up to the mark. There was only one who made good, and that was Yuan Mei. I hear it was you who passed him. I am glad there is someone who puts me in countenance.'

Chiang P'u was, we are told, particularly delighted to be backed up in this way because 'Ortai and Chiang P'u's father both took their Second Degree in the same year (1699)'. This sentence admirably illustrates the curious social bond which united examination-comrades, and even extended into the next generation. But if Chiang P'u was delighted, the same (Yuan Mei tells us) cannot be said of Chao Kuo-lin and the other examiners, who 'exchanged surprised glances'. 'I should have liked', Yuan continues, 'to have called upon Lord Ortai and thanked him; but owing to his high rank I did not dare to do so.'

An important friendship which he made at this time was with Chiang Ho-ning (1707–1784), who was at that time living with the Emperor's cousin Prince Ning: 'Whenever he left the Forbidden City, he spent the night with me. We were neither of us drinkers and both of us were fond of talking about the past. We trimmed the candles and sat opposite one another, discussing the ups and downs of national affairs during the last three thousand years, appraising all the outstanding figures and, when we found ourselves in particularly close agreement on some disputed point, thumping on our stools and shouting with delight, even more pleased with each other than before. And my servant, whenever he heard that Mr. Chiang was coming, knowing how late we should sit up, laid in a great stock of dip-candles.' The phrase I have translated 'trimming candles' means literally 'breaking off the char'. Old-fashioned Chinese candles have wicks of wood or bamboo from which the char has to be broken off at intervals.

From this friendship, which endured for fifty years, Yuan Mei's interest in history and the methods of historical research gained much stimulus; and from it he may also have obtained interesting lights on the young Emperor's private life and habits.

To this period, too, belongs his friendship with the young actor Hsü Yun-t'ing. 'All the Han-lin scholars were crazy about him and clubbed together to pay for theatricals in which he appeared. I was young and good-looking, but I was so poorly accoutred that I did not think Yun-t'ing could possibly regard me as worth cultivating. But I noticed on one occasion that he often glanced my way and smiled, quite with the air of indicating that he had taken a fancy to me. I hardly dared to believe this and did not try to get into touch with him. However, very early next day I heard a knock at my door. There he was; and we were soon on the most affectionate terms—a state of affairs all the more delightful, because it far exceeded anything I had expected.' He addressed elaborate and allusive poems to Yun-t'ing and to one or two other boy-actors. Neither now, however, nor at any other period of his life was he exclusively interested in men.

In the winter of 1739, probably at the bidding of his parents, he obtained leave to go home and marry Miss Wang, to whom, as I have said, he had long been affianced. She was twenty-two, a very late age at which to get married, most girls of her class marrying at fourteen or fifteen. He tells us that when he arrived in his home in Hangchow all his friends and relatives pressed round him, as he stood there in his Court dress, pouring out pæans of congratulation and delight. ' "How proud of you your mother must be", they all said. But strangely enough it was only my mother who remained completely unaffected and, without a word about my success, still treated me as though I were a child.' About his wife we hear very little. We know that later on she nursed him devotedly when he was ill and that she outlived him by some years; but that is all. On his return to Peking he was ordered to take a course in the Manchu language and script. There was, during the whole of the Manchu dynasty (1644–1912), a strong undercurrent of hostility to the foreign regime, especially among members of the old bureaucratic families. Some of them had, on the fall of the native Ming dynasty, emigrated to Japan; many struggled on in circumstances of great difficulty rather than accept office from their conquerors. There were certainly, in the middle of the eighteenth century, still many scholars who felt it as an indignity to be compelled to learn a barbarous foreign language and script. There is, however, no reason to suppose that Yuan Mei had any such feeling. He enjoyed, as we have seen, the patronage and friendship of some of the most influential and cultivated Manchus of the day, and he even went so far as to say, towards the end of his life, that 'nowadays the Manchus are much more cultivated than the Chinese. Even their military men all write poetry'. And he cited the case of K'uei-lun, a Manchu general then commanding in Fukhien, who practised the art of 'finger-tip' painting and wrote elegant verse inscriptions on his pictures.

The teaching of the Han-lin scholars was in the hands of the President of the Board of Punishments, Shih I-chih (1682–1763), whose attention was caught by a practice 'Memorial to the Throne' which Yuan Mei had written during a day off from Manchu lessons. He soon formed the habit of slipping unannounced into the President's study and was regaled by him with a copious flow of information about the institutes of the Manchu regime, the political achievements of the two preceding reigns, and anecdotes about the signal marks of favour that the President had received from three successive Emperors. His actual tutor in Manchu was a certain Tsou T'ai-ho, who had entered the Han-lin Academy in 1718: 'He was an affable, unassuming man, with an extraordinary passion for cats. Whenever he gave a party his grandchild and his cat were always at his side. When he gave a tit-bit to his grandchild, he always gave an exactly similar portion to his cat. "It's the only way to ensure that there is no snatching", he said. He was once made Inspector of Education in Honan and after his inspection at Shang-ch'iu, in that province, when he left his headquarters, his cat was nowhere to be found. He ordered the authorities at Shang-ch'iu to make the most exhaustive search; but the Prefect, to save himself trouble, simply sent in the usual printed formula used in reporting unsuccessful searches for missing persons, filling in the word "cat" by hand: "In view of your Exalted Instructions four persons from this prefecture have carried out an exhaustive search in contiguous residences; but though the time-limit has expired, Your Excellency's CAT has not been found".'

His Manchu studies continued during the next year (1741) and were a subject of mirth to his greatest friend at this period, Ch'iu Yueh-hsiu (1712–1773), who 'laughed at the heavy work I made of reading those "tadpole scripts"'. Ch'iu lured him from his studies to play draughts and read the *Sou Shen Chi*, a reputedly fourth-century A.D. collection of wonder stories. He also took him to pay court to Ts'ai-yü, a famous singing-girl from Anhwei.

The examination of the Han-lin scholars took place in the spring of next year (1742). The papers of those who had been assigned to the study of Manchu were read by Yuan Mei's Manchu friend and patron, Ortai. To prevent favouritism the names of the candidates had a slip pasted over them, which the examiner was only allowed to remove after he had marked the papers. It was with chagrin that Ortai discovered, after placing a set of papers in the lowest possible category, the name of Yuan Mei under the pasted slip. 'He sent for me, gave me dinner and then discussed my future very seriously. "When the Emperor sees you", he said, "I am sure that your appearance alone will make him anxious to use you. I do not doubt that as a provincial official you would show yourself perfectly competent. Some people look upon you solely as a literary man and think this renders you unfit to be an official. But I know you better than that." ' After the examination the candidates were presented to the Emperor and the young man who could not learn Manchu knelt at the feet of the Manchu Emperor—

'*only three feet away from Heaven*'.

He was ordered to go to Nanking and report to the authorities there, with a view to becoming Prefect of some district in that region. In 1743, at the early age of 27, he became Prefect of Li-shui, about 50 miles south-east of Nanking. On his way south from Peking he made a detour in order to climb the T'ai-shan, the highest mountain in China proper (4,500 feet). 'Climb' is perhaps as little suitable in this case as it is to the ascents of those modern athletes who do their mountaineering in funiculars and on ski-lifts; for he was carried up in a basket slung on ropes, lying coiled up in it 'like a silkworm', by two coolies who sidled up the stone causeway 'like veritable crabs'.

CHAPTER THREE

Prefect

HIS appointment at Li-shui and his subsequent appointment at Chiang-pu were, he tells us, both due to the Manchu Prince Te-p'ei (1688–1752), who in 1742 and 1743 was Governor-General of Kiangsi and Kiangnan. The prince was a man of great seriousness, an ascetic ardently devoted to Confucianism. Yuan Mei wrote an obituary of him in which he says: 'His complexion was ruddy and he had no beard or moustache. His chin jutted out sharp as an arrow and he had all the air of a rigid philosopher. He was waited upon solely by Palace eunuchs, and when he interviewed lower officials everyone from the head eunuch downward had to remain kneeling while they spoke. His own conversation turned exclusively upon Goodness and Right, as taught by the Duke of Chou and Confucius. When he heard good of anyone he always believed it; when he heard evil, he doubted. He was affable in his manner towards all his officials; but if he found that any of them understood the Classics or showed a special talent for administration he became most affectionate and treated them more like disciples than subordinates. . . . When I was Prefect of Chiang-p'u, he happened to pass through the place and his attendants insisted on inordinate preparations being made for his reception. I informed him of this and he gave strict orders on the subject. After that his staff kept very quiet. From that time onward he showed that he had a great regard for me.'

About 1718 the German Jesuit missionary Ignatius Kögler baptized an unnamed Manchu prince. From the particulars given it seems clear that this prince was Te-p'ei. It has even been maintained that Te-p'ei's published writings show Christian influence. The passages cited by the Chinese Catholic historian Ch'en Yuan do not seem to me to contain anything specifically Christian. But one would have to be far more familiar with the byways of eighteenth-century Confucianism than I am, to decide whether his ideas (for example about the mortal body and immortal soul) are such as no parallel could be found for inside contemporary Confucianism. In a poem about him Yuan wrote:

Lecturers are mostly commonplace Confucians;
But in him one feels at once the touch of distinction.
And if one asks, why is he so different?—
One truth drives out a hundred shams.

I was tempted at first to write 'One Truth' and to suppose that Yuan is referring to Te-p'ei's Christianity; but I doubt if that is what he meant. My impression is that Te-p'ei was probably a practising Christian only for a few years, but the whole subject is very obscure.

His father, who was living at Kuei-lin, soon joined him at Li-shui. In a later poem he says of his father:

He was worried about my still being so young
And doubted whether I was capable of doing my job.
So on entering my district he put on a wide-brimmed hat,
Disguising himself as a peasant on the tramp.
He gathered about him the village gaffers and dames,
Asking them what sort of Prefect they had.
They said 'He is a young man from the Han-lin
Who does not seem to be more than twenty-eight.
But he settles disputes with great wisdom and firmness,
And his disposition is most friendly and kind'.
In every village it was the same story;
Words of praise never left their lips.

Having heard their tale, without changing his dress
He rode on his donkey straight up to my house.
None of my people had known him in old days;
But, somewhat bewildered, they hastened to bring him in.
I thought he would be cross at my not going to meet him,
And knelt before him, my heart full of dread.
But on the contrary he seemed very pleased,
And proceeded at once to tell me all that he had heard.
He said, 'The news that you are doing so well
Is a better welcome than the costliest meats and drinks'.
But that night we did have extra dishes
And laughed and laughed throughout the whole meal.
I have never been happy about my treatment of my father,
And am often beset with feelings of remorse.
Only from the thought of what happened then
Do I sometimes get a whiff of consolation. . . .

At the Han-lin there had been a free and easy atmosphere; seniors and juniors mixed together almost on an equality. But in the provinces the higher magistrates demanded from their subordinates a vast deal of punctilio. Yuan Mei found it hard to remember that in writing to superiors he must sign his name and rank in minute characters, lest he should seem to claim equality with the person he was writing to; and that when appearing before these great men he must sink to his knees noiselessly, the least sound being interpreted as an impertinence. He took his new duties very seriously, determined to be a model official. From the 'Taoist Paradise' of the Han-lin he had 'descended into the world of men', unsure what awaited him. The retiring Prefect was not encouraging. He told him that the region was particularly hard to administer. There was famine already, and as the crops had been badly damaged earlier in the year, there were misgivings about the next harvest. Crowds of angry women were holding up the officials' coaches, clambering on to the shafts and cursing them for their exactions.

He was only at Li-shui for a few months, and almost the

only story of his official dealings there is the following romantic episode: 'There was a girl of good family who lived with her grandmother. She had an affair with her nephew, a man called Ch'en. They eloped together, but were caught and brought to me for punishment. It was at the height of summer, and while the woman knelt before me in the blazing sun the sweat poured down her cheeks, which gave a dazzling gleam to her complexion. The man Ch'en, a leather-worker by trade, was hideous. I could not help thinking of the lines, "A handsome mate I sought, but got this toad!" I could not understand what had possessed her to go off with such a man. When I asked her to make a statement she said weeping, "What happened must be due to the *karma* of some previous incarnation. Otherwise how could I have suffered a momentary infatuation to bring this shame to my ancestors?" The grandmother was in a great rage; I remonstrated with her mildly, ordered the nephew to be thrashed, and sent the girl home.' The lines about 'a handsome mate I sought' are from No. 43 in *The Book of Songs*, China's earliest anthology.

He was soon transferred for a few months to Chiang-p'u, a place close to Nanking, but on the far side of the river, and then to Shu-yang, far away in northern Kiangsu, near the borders of Shantung province. Some time during this year (1743), only four years after his marriage, he took a Miss T'ao to live with him as concubine. She was 'clever at draughts and embroidery' and could also play on her zither (*ch'in*) the melancholy ballad *Ch'u Ming Kuang*, about a Minister who in the fifth century B.C. was falsely accused of treachery. Yuan Mei's wife had borne him no children, and it may have been partly for this reason that he took a concubine. But I am inclined to think that his wife (chosen for him when both the parties were mere children) did not attract him physically, and that he added Miss T'ao to his household chiefly because he had taken a fancy to her.

In 1743, following upon devastating floods, there was a long drought. There was some attempt at official famine relief. Those who pushed and scrambled successfully at the place of distribution got enough rice to eke out a lean existence for a few weeks. Many got nothing at all. Morning and evening Yuan Mei burnt incense and called upon Heaven to send rain. There was no hope for the main harvest, but some late-sown corn might still be saved, and he gave orders for the Rain Dragons to be carried in procession. Two days later, on the twenty-third day of the sixth month, rain at last fell.

At Shu-yang people suffered a great deal from ulcers, which (though the sea is at least fifty miles away) Yuan Mei attributed to the unwholesome effect of sea-air. He had an attack in the spring, from which he soon recovered. But late in the autumn he had a bad relapse, for which he was treated with sulphide of arsenic and an extract of cocklebur.

At Shu-yang there was no granary at which the people could deposit the grain that the government exacted as taxation in kind. The nearest was over thirty miles away. The rich, of course, brought it in wagons or in sacks carried by pack-horses; but the poor had to carry it in baskets strapped to their backs. The Manchu soldiers in charge of grain-transport demanded a standard of grain such as did not exist after the recent floods and drought. The poem that Yuan Mei wrote about this, 'in order that my Sovereign may know', does not manage to rise above being anything but rhymed prose. Regarded, however, simply as a pamphlet, it has great eloquence.

In the autumn of 1744 he was one of the assistant examiners in the Provincial Examinations at Nanking. Despite the fact that in the preceding year some signs of a beard had begun to appear on his chin, he felt that the chief examiner regarded him as ridiculously young, and explained that he had already worn Court dress for six years. As one who had so recently had the bitter experience of failing in four examinations, he found it hard to bring himself to reject candidates:

When the lists go up much is heard of the candidates' resentment;
No one realizes with what sadness the examiners did their duty.

He found one essay on a subject from the Five Classics which, in his opinion, stood head and shoulders above the rest. He marked it as outstanding; but the chief examiner waved his hand and said that the 'fixed number' had already been reached, and was annoyed when Yuan Mei continued to press the candidate's claims.

I knew well enough that the 'fixed number' rule is hard to break;
But wondered how many included in the number were this fellow's match.

Examination results, he concludes, depend on Fate (or, as we should say, luck), not on literary ability; and he quotes the case of the great poet Su Tung-p'o who in A.D. 1057 was beaten in the examinations by a certain Li Fang-shu, of whom no one has ever heard. The 'fixed number' refers to the rule that only a specified number of candidates from any one district could be passed.

In this year there took place in his family two events which greatly concerned him. The news arrived (very belatedly, owing to a previous letter having gone astray), that the uncle with whom he stayed at Kuei-lin eight years ago and to whom he was deeply attached, had died there in 1740. Yuan Mei's brother Yuan Shu, who later became a fairly well-known painter, was living with the uncle at Kuei-lin, and as soon as Yuan Mei heard the news he sent for the brother (then a boy of fourteen) and installed him at his parents' house at Hangchow.

The other event was the marriage of his sister Su-wen, four years younger than himself. The story of the marriage is a strange one. Years ago, in 1723, when Su-wen was four, a friend of old Mr. Yuan named Kao, to whose family Mr. Yuan had done a good turn, offered as fiancé to Su-wen the child with whom his wife was then pregnant, in the event of its being a boy. After that Yuan Mei's father, wandering from one small post to another in western and southern China, lost touch with the Kao family. At last, in 1742, when Yuan Mei's father was again living with his family in Hangchow, a messenger arrived from the Kaos, saying that Su-wen's fiancé was ill, and that the marriage could not take place. The girl was now twenty-two, and it would have been difficult to find her another husband; for a girl of that age was already considered completely *passée*. But an invalid husband was not an encouraging prospect, and Yuan Mei's father was at a loss how to reply. However, 'my sister, her gilded engagement necklet in her hand, wept and would not eat; my father wept and would not eat', and the messenger appears to have brought back the news that the Yuan family regarded the engagement as still holding good. Su-wen's constancy to an ailing fiancé was much lauded by the Kaos and their friends. In 1742 old Mr. Kao died, and a nephew of his arrived with the surprising intelligence that the fiancé had never been ill at all. 'What happened was this', explained the nephew. 'The young man was guilty of "bestial conduct". My uncle beat him "to death", but he came to life again. However, he felt that to let your daughter marry him would be a poor way of requiting your services to our family and he therefore invented the story about his illness as an excuse for breaking off the engagement. The young lady need not afflict herself.'

'Bestial conduct' means incest. The term had a very wide range, including (as one would expect) intercourse with a sister by the same mother, with a paternal cousin, and with the wife of a brother. But, as incest, too, was reckoned intercourse with one's father's or grandfather's concubine, either of whom might, of course, have been quite young. From a Western point of view it certainly seems very strange that Yuan senior should have accepted as his son-in-law a man whom he had never seen and about whom he knew nothing except that he had committed incest. Yuan Mei makes no comment; to do so would have involved criticizing his father, which was not permissible. The bridegroom turned out to be 'dwarfish, hunch-backed and cross-eyed. He had a vile temper and when it was roused behaved in the most outrageous way. It angered him to see my sister use her brush, and she gave up writing poetry. It angered him to see her sew, and she gave up her embroidery. He used to look through her jewel-case, take her small possessions and sell them to pay for his debaucheries. If he found nothing, he would fly into a temper, smash her things, stamp upon them and burn them. There was no outrage he would not commit. Once his mother tried to intervene; whereupon he struck her and broke her teeth. When my sister found that he was planning to sell her into slavery to pay his gambling debts, she saw that the situation was hopeless, and wrote to my father who, in a towering rage, went to the magistrate and got the marriage annulled.' One child was born, a girl afflicted with dumbness, whom the unhappy Su-wen taught to communicate in writing. Su-wen's presence in the house cannot have added much to its gaiety, for we are told that after her divorce she 'only wore the drabbest clothes, gave up dressing her hair, would not listen to music, and on festival-days sat weeping with her back turned on the merry-makers'.

On returning to Shu-yang he heard that the district was about to be visited by a provincial inspector named Chuang Heng-yang (1686–1746). 'It was reported', he says, 'that Chuang was a strict Neo-Confucian, and I felt uneasy about his visit, expecting him to be haughty and unapproachable. When he arrived, the usual banquet of welcome was prepared for him and to my surprise he did not refuse a single dish, saying "I never refuse what has already been cooked. To do so is a rebuff to Heaven, who has given us these good things, and to the kind thought of those who offer them. Good manners demand that the guest should eat whatever his host eats". After the meal he made me stay and drink with him. After the third cup he began to question me in great detail about local conditions at Shu-yang—the river-conservancy measures, the state of local finances. The talk then went on to geography, astronomy, music, on all of which he spoke with excellent judgment. He finally showed me some of his poems, which were remarkably skilful. Next day he visited the school and gave a talk about *The Doctrine of the Mean* (Chung-yung), not treating the boys to a mere smattering of Sung Confucian maxims, but explaining the ideas of the work with absolute clarity and precision, so that the countenances of his hearers visibly changed while he spoke, as though for the first time they were aboard a chariot that was bound for the realms of true wisdom. Whatever questions were asked, however crudely put, he listened to without the slightest sign of impatience. The day after that, there was an inspection of the local volunteers. They cut a very poor figure both in archery and with their matchlocks, hitting only the rim of the target or missing it altogether, and burning their fingers when they set the fuses of their guns. They ended by flinging themselves at the feet of the Inspector and begging for forgiveness. I, meanwhile, stood by in fear and trembling, trying as best I could to make excuses for the elementary state of their training. But all the Inspector did was to take off his outer coat, come forward bow in hand and then, "propping the left arm and crooking the right arm", he put them through their paces to such effect that soon there was not one in the squad of eighteen who did not hit the bull's-eye; and the musket-firing went equally well. When it was over he sat down and said to me with a smile, "There's no need for you to look so downcast. It is quite a normal thing for literary men, after they have learnt that job, not to train themselves in other directions. It is just to take this sort of thing off your hands that I come every year on my round of inspection." '

In 1745, through the influence of his Manchu patron Yin-chi-shan, Yuan Mei was transferred to Nanking, where he was Prefect of what one might call one of the constituent boroughs of the city. The position was a much more responsible and important one than his post at Shu-yang, and no doubt he was kept pretty busy:

Morning after morning at the fifth watch I climb into my carriage;
I must pay my respects to those above me, meet them, see them off,

Answer the questions of their clients and guests while time flies away.
The inner wall of Nanking is sixty leagues round,
To do the whole circuit of the town is about a day's job.
When at last I manage to get home the lamps are beginning to be lit;
Through the dusk I trundle to the fold, as do the cows and sheep.
Women folk holding their brats block the entry to my house,
And while the children tug at my skirts their elders make excuses:
'We all said what a pity it was that you were kept so late;
It never occurred to anyone that you had not had your supper.'
Gasping with hunger, yet holding out, I put my papers in order;
Just on the verge of reaching a decision I go back again to the start.
I am haunted by the fear that further delay may do harm to my people;
Yet I know well that when I hurry I make a lot of mistakes.
The tangled threads are straightened out; at last I am leaving my office
When a young Bachelor turns up, and wants to show me an essay:
'Knowing that your Worship was previously employed in the Han-lin Academy
I felt I should not be doing my duty if I did not pay my respects.'

The poem goes on to tell how far into the night reports of matters requiring urgent attention continue to pour in: owing to the negligence of the gaolers, several prisoners have escaped; the public granary-keepers have allowed an inch of rot to spread over the corn, and finally, when Yuan Mei has at last got to bed and is fast asleep, there is a knock at the door, and someone announces that a fire has broken out. 'The Prefect's attendance is urgently requested.'

His disturbed night has its compensation, for at the fire he met 'a beautiful young man in an unlined silk robe. He had an air of great elegance and refinement, and I was much struck by him. On enquiring who he was, I was told he was a Bachelor, named Kung Ju-chang. Next day he called upon me, bringing some things he had written, and I made great friends with him. Ten years later he took his Third Degree and changed his name to Kung Sun-chih.' But the exigencies of public service made friendship hard to maintain. Kung Sun-chih became Prefect of a district near T'ai-yuan, far away to the north, and we last hear of him patriotically cooking mutton for hungry troops marching to the conquest of Turkestan, about 1756.

There are many anecdotes about the humanity and common sense displayed by Yuan Mei in his work as a magistrate at Nanking. We are told by his grandson Yuan Tsu-chih (1827–1898) that these were collected in a book called *Sui-yuan Kung-an* (i.e. Yuan Mei's Legal Decisions), which had a wide circulation. The grandson also tells us that a number of play-ballads were made, 'of a very laughable kind', called 'The Decision about the Centipede', 'The Decision about the Donkey', 'The Decision about the Fowl', 'The Decision about the Basket', and performed at street-corners. In a poem of 1795 Yuan Mei himself says:

Do not quote the ditties of chairmen about those old days—
Idle rumours handed down for the last fifty years.

And he adds the note, 'Ballad-singers in the market-places still twang tales about my good rule when I was Prefect at Nanking. But they are all pure concoctions, much like the apocryphal "Life of the magician Tung-fang So".' The anecdotes about his legal decisions (as opposed to the popular ballads) found their way into the various short biographical sketches of his life that still exist. They are typical of the sort of tales that were commonly told about model magistrates, and even if to some extent founded on fact, they cannot be unreservedly accepted as history. But they represent practically all that the average person knows about Yuan Mei's early life today; just as the story about the burning of the cakes is all that most of us know about King Alfred. One such story is that two families had been engaged in endless litigation about the ownership of a piece of land. A file of depositions and counter-depositions was laid before him when the case came on again. 'If things go on like this', he said, 'you will both be ruined. Let me wind up the case for you.' He then tossed aside the whole ancient dossier, portioned the disputed fields and gave each of the disputants a new lease; with the result that the land was again put under cultivation and the taxes on it flowed into the Treasury. Chinese magistrates had indeed very wide powers of discretion in such cases. The principle of *i* (common sense, reason) could always be applied if it was obvious that a strict application of the laws of the land would be deleterious to all concerned, and even junior officials were able on their own initiative to make sensible though illegal decisions without waiting (as they would have to do in England) for a special Act of Parliament.

On another occasion, it is said, a ship on which a cloth-merchant was transporting his wares collided with a naval craft manned by soldiers, and one soldier was drowned. The remaining soldiers bound the crew of the merchant ship and brought them for trial, making the merchant come along too. Yuan Mei knew that if he gave a judgment of accidental homicide the fines would have to be paid by the merchant, who would be completely ruined. So he handled the case merely as one of a collision between ships, and said to the sailors and merchant, 'You had better hoist sail while the wind holds'. He then gave the soldiers some money with which to pay for their comrade's funeral, and declared that the case was closed.

In the summer of 1745 a Mr. Li came to Yuan's office saying that his young son's wife had disappeared and had subsequently turned up at a village some thirty miles distant from Nanking. He asked that his son should be allowed to divorce her, on the ground that it was obvious she must have gone there to join a lover. The wife denied this and said that she had been caught up by the great typhoon on the tenth of the fifth month and carried by it to this village.

Mr. Li refused to believe the story; but Yuan Mei, evidently anxious to prevent the girl from getting into trouble, pointed out that there was a case on record of a woman being blown to a place over a thousand miles away: 'I sent for the Works of Hao Ching (1223–1275) and showed him the story. "Hao Ching", I said, "was the most faithful of Kubla Khan's ministers, and we are bound to believe what he tells us. As you see, the girl in that case ended by marrying a Prime Minister. I only wish I could promise you that your son will get as far as that." The Governor-General, Yin-chi-shan, when he heard of this said, "That only shows how important it is that Prefects should be men of wide reading!" ' The only available edition of Hao Ching's Works is an abridgment representing little more than half of the original. In it the story about the lady who was blown a thousand miles is not to be found; but no doubt it may be found in the complete edition, which still exists. This, it should be remarked, is a story that Yuan Mei tells himself, and not one of the legends that were told in later days about his career as Prefect of Nanking.

Early next year he renewed a literary friendship made under curious circumstances: 'When I was conducting the Boys' Examination at Shu-yang, a certain Master Chou showed me an essay which seemed to me so good that I could hardly believe that it was his own work. I made enquiries and found that it was really by the boy's teacher, a graduate of Huai-an, called Lü Wen-kuang. I treated him with such politeness and took so much trouble in polishing up his essays that everyone thought I was entertaining some influential guest. Not long afterwards I was moved to Nanking and had been there a year or so when someone in full scholastic robes came up to my carriage and saluted me. He turned out to be Lü Wen-kuang. I asked him what I could do for him and he told me that since I left Shu-yang he had gone on with his studies, but very much felt the lack of anyone to guide him; so he had thrown up his tutoring job and come to me at Nanking. I was delighted by his enthusiasm and arranged with the authorities to give him access to the Provincial library, at the same time inviting him to come to my official residence and become tutor to my two orphaned nephews. As soon as I was through with my day's business, he used to come to me with his writings. I was perfectly frank with him and criticized them quite mercilessly. When I thought them unworthy of him I told him so in the strongest possible language and sometimes even went so far as to tear them up and throw them on the ground. Lü Wen-kuang would then pick up the fragments without showing the slightest resentment and spend the rest of the night in hacking them about. When he waited upon me next day, he looked perfectly brisk and fresh.' In 1753 Lü Wen-kuang married a sister of Yuan Mei's wife, clad in a red robe lent to him by Yuan. In 1754, when Yuan was gravely ill with malaria, Lü lavished upon him the tenderest devotion, but was too emotional to be an ideal sick-nurse, for 'he was in such distress about me that he could scarcely control his movements. He was indeed so unsteady in his gait that he walked straight into my screen and with a sweep of his arm upset the lamp.' Afterwards he became Prefect of a district in Honan (1757) and wrote offering to devote part of his salary to pay for the printing of a collection of topographical poems and essays by Yuan Mei. 'Let us wait', replied Yuan, 'till I am older and wiser, and you are richer than you are now.' Lü was planning to retire from his official post and come to live near Yuan, when he fell ill and died. For some twenty years he was Yuan's most devoted follower and closest friend.

To the next year (1747) belongs a poem on the destruction by fire of an ancient and celebrated Gingko (maidenhair tree):

At depth of night there is a cry of birds and the sky suddenly glows.
On the bare hill there are no houses; the light is in a tree!
Torn shoots rise and scatter in clouds of yellow gold;
From the Nine Heavens ashes pour; the thick smoke curls.

Bursting and crackling in the darkened wind its heart's
blood runs dry;
Branch on branch and leaf on leaf flake the snowless sky.
Root and branches, alive and dead, share one breath;
Blazing it falls straight down, three thousand feet.

The poet then goes on to imagine (less vividly) how the tree had been planted a thousand and more years ago in the garden of some vanished palace, and had survived the centuries for the very reason that it was so tall, and builders preferred shorter trunks, which were not so much trouble to saw into beams and rafters of the right length. The poem closes with the reflection that the crows and magpies need not lament so clamorously; it is all in the day's work for their nests to be burnt and their mansions to topple over; but

The old monk lingers sadly beside his favourite tree.;
Henceforward where will he seek shelter from the rain and sun?

In the summer of 1747 Yin-chi-shan, who was at this time acting Governor-General of Kiangsi and Kiangnan, recommended Yuan Mei as Governor of Kao-yu, near Yangchow, a far more important post than the one he held at Nanking. But the Board of Civil Office would not sanction the promotion.

At the beginning of 1748 when on the way to Soochow to pay his New Year respects to Yin-chi-shan he stayed at the house of a friend called T'ang Ching-han, who gave a party to which he brought a dazzling collection of Soochow beauties. But in Yuan Mei's opinion they were all eclipsed by a girl who turned out to be one of Mr. T'ang's house-servants. 'So you think she is pretty?' said Mr. T'ang. 'In that case she and all her charms are yours from now onwards.' So Fang Tsung (for that was her name) became Yuan Mei's second concubine. He had already inspected another girl on his way to Soochow. A Mr. Li, who was temporary Prefect at

Yangchow, had written saying that there was a girl called Wang, with whom he had had dealings at his office and whom he should like to present to Yuan Mei as a concubine. 'Hiring a boat I went to Yangchow and saw the girl at the shrine of Kuan-yin, where she was living with her mother. She was eighteen and had a very good figure. She let me look her up and down, draw back her dress and lift the hair from her temples without seeming to resent it in the least. I had half a mind to take her. But her complexion was not quite up to the mark, and I gave up the idea. After I got to Soochow I sent someone to have another look at her; but some minor official of Kiangnan had already got hold of her.' This is not Yuan Mei at his most edifying!

Later in 1748 he applied for 'sick leave'. This was a recognized way of resigning from a post and at the same time having three months' pay in hand. If at the end of three months' sick-leave (during which he received full pay) an official did not go back to work, he automatically lost his job.

In the autumn a friend called T'ao Shih-huang who had been Provincial Treasurer at Ch'ang-sha, south of the Yangtze, and was now going to take up a post in Fuhkien, passed through Nanking and was distressed to hear of Yuan Mei's intention to retire. 'You have just had the distinction', he said, 'of being considered for the post of Governor at Kao-yu, you are not much over thirty, and yet you suddenly declare your intention of abandoning your official career. I cannot understand how a man of your parts can be so foolish.' After thinking the matter over, he wrote to T'ao denying that (as T'ao had evidently asserted) he was resigning because he considered it an indignity to serve as a Prefect after having been a scholar in the Han-lin Academy, or because he was piqued at failing to get the Governorship of Kao-yu. He goes on to say that the work of a Prefect in a large town consists chiefly of dancing attendance on higher officials, 'which I am very bad at', and not on straightening out the difficulties of ordinary people, 'which I do very well'. He then describes a day in his official life in much the same terms as in the poem quoted above, and he ends by saying (perhaps rather rhetorically), 'All I ask for is a village of some ten houses where I could live exactly as I chose, and rule the people merely by chanting to them the Way of the Former Kings; then I could end my days there in perfect contentment, even though I only ranked as a village constable. But as for coursing about the blazing streets of a great town—all I can say is that not even the strong-men Meng Pen and Hsia Yü could have done it without an occasional rest under the shade of a tree. All I ask for is to be allowed to take such a rest, and you ought not to blame me.' The statement that he was not piqued at having been refused the job at Kao-yu was probably untrue. At any rate in his Will (1797) he says, 'The Board of Civil Office failed to sanction the appointment. I was piqued and asked for leave.'

Giving up his post of course involved losing his official residence, and he had now to look round for somewhere to live. For three hundred ounces of silver (one month's salary; £100 at the then rate of exchange) he bought a piece of ground formerly attached to the villa of a Mr. Sui, who had been the Superintendant of the Imperial Textile Factory at Nanking. After Sui's death the place had been left deserted. What remained of the villa had become a tavern, and the garden was completely overgrown. It pleased Yuan Mei to identify the site with one which, a thousand years ago, the great poet Li Po had coveted. He went on hunting for literary associations, and some thirty years later he persuaded himself that his garden was the one described by Ts'ao Chan in *The Dream of the Red Chamber*, the most famous of all Chinese novels. It is true that the Ts'ao family had owned the villa before (*c.* 1728) it passed into the hands of Mr. Sui. But Ts'ao Chan's book, though partly autobiographical, is fiction not history, the garden in the novel is now generally thought to be based on one at Peking, and it seems to lie in a very different type of landscape.

The ground was so steep and uneven that it would have been difficult to wall it in. No attempt at any sort of barrier was put up and holiday-makers were allowed to wander about the grounds in perfect freedom, as long as they kept at a reasonable distance from the living quarters. A feature of the garden, perhaps surviving from old days, was a high mirador, from which one could see approaching guests long before they arrived:

Don't laugh at my tower being so high;
Think what pleasure I shall gain from its being so high!
I shall not have to wait till you arrive;
I shall see you clearly ten leagues away!
But when you come, do not come in your coach;
The sound of a coach scares my birds away.
When you come do not ride your horse;
For it might be hungry and try its teeth on my plants.
When you come, don't come too early;
We country people stay late in bed.
But when you come, don't come too late;
For late in the day the flowers are not at their best.

The Sui Yuan, Yuan Mei's residence, when finished, consisted of twenty-four pavilions, standing separately in the grounds, or built round small courtyards. Behind the pavilions was a piece of artificial water, divided into two parts by a meandering causeway, with little humped bridges that enabled a boat to pass from one part of the lake to the other. It was a miniature imitation of the causeways over the Western Lake at Hangchow. At the western end of the artificial water was another miniature imitation—that of the Ch'i-hsia Monastery at Nanking, which was fitted up as a temporary palace when Ch'ien Lung visited the South in 1751, a fact which was officially supposed greatly to have augmented its holiness. It was Yin-chi-shan who suggested that the Emperor should lodge at the Ch'i-hsia, and Yin-chi-shan who wrote the inscription 'Little Ch'i-hsia' that hung above the entrance to Yuan Mei's miniature replica.

CHAPTER FOUR

At the Sui-yuan, and Journey to the North-West

HE vacated his *yamen* at Nanking on the fourth day of the first month (1749) and went to Hangchow, having heard that his mother was ailing. His wife and two concubines had preceded him. One of the concubines, Miss T'ao, had recently borne him his first child, a daughter called A-ch'eng. He wrote a long poem describing his visit to Hangchow in an elaborately allusive and crabbed style, which perhaps reflects his uneasiness at finding himself surrounded by almost forgotten relatives. He says indeed that the Hangchow dialect, which he had not heard for so long, at first bewildered him. Before he left, his wife opened 'two blue boxes' and gave him some of her jewellery to sell, saying that apart from this he had nothing to live on but his writings. He took back with him to Nanking, presumably to camp uncomfortably in some ruined pavilion of the garden, his younger brother, Yuan Shu, and his elder sister's son Lu Chien.

In the winter of 1749 he fell ill and was cured by a remarkable doctor called Hsueh I-p'iao. There were, at the time, two main schools of medicine in China. The traditionalists (of whom the most celebrated was Hsu Ta-ch'un, 1693–1771) used supposedly ancient treatises, in some cases believed to date from several millennia B.C.; the modernists (of whom Hsueh I-p'iao, *c.* 1681–1775, was one of the foremost) paid more attention to later works which embodied the experience of practising physicians. The Chinese constantly coupled together the names 'physician' and 'shaman' (*wu*). Indeed, the two terms became more or less a single word, meaning healers in general. Both alike were to some extent looked down upon by strict Confucians, and it is common to read in funeral eulogies that in his last illness the deceased 'showed great fortitude and refused to let himself be treated by doctors or shamans'. The fact that Hsueh I-p'iao was a 'modernist' by no means implied that his bed-side manner was that of a scientist rather than that of a wonder-worker. Here is a picture of Hsueh I-p'iao at work. 'Once when I was at Soochow my cook Wang Hsiao-yü was stricken down with smallpox and became unconscious. We had given him up for lost, when late at night Dr. Hsueh arrived. He lit a candle and holding it over him he said, "He is dead; but I am no bad hand at wrestling with the smallpox demon. I am not sure, but I rather think I shall win." He then brought out a pill, pounded it up with stone-flag (*acorus gramineus*), and asked us to send for a very muscular litter-bearer. When the man arrived, he gave him an iron poker and told him to force open the jaws of the patient, who still lay unconscious, with closed eyes. Dr. Hsueh then poured his mixture down the patient's throat, and there was a gurgling sound as though he were swallowing it and bringing it up again. "Let someone keep an eye on him", said Dr. Hsueh. "By cock-crow he should recover the power of speech." And so it turned out. He was given two more doses, and completely recovered.'

Another story of Dr. Hsueh's powers concerns a strange case of 'possession'. 'In the fifteenth year of Ch'ien Lung (1750) when I was staying with Chiang Liang-feng at Soochow, his son Chiang Pao-ch'en, on returning from the Provincial Examinations at Nanking, became seriously ill. Chiang summoned a host of famous doctors from far and near, but they appeared all to be completely baffled. He knew that I was on friendly terms with Dr. Hsueh and insisted upon my writing to him and asking him to come. Chiang and I were standing at the gate waiting for Hsueh to come when inside the house we heard the patient call out "Here's Mr. Ku Yao-nien!", and then "That's right, Mr. Ku; take a seat". Ku Yao-nien was a citizen of Soochow who had incited the mob to thrash an official as a protest against the high price of rice, and had been executed by Lord An, the Governor of Soochow. The ghost apparently took a seat, and we heard him saying, "Well, Master Chiang! You've passed your examination. Your name is thirty-eighth on the list. This illness of yours is nothing to worry about. You can get rid of it any time by giving me meat and wine. Do that, and I'll go away at once." Hearing this, the young man's father rushed into his room and tried to soothe him by saying, "Mr. Ku will soon go away; we're going to make an offering to him immediately". But the ghost (speaking through the sick man's mouth) said, "There's that Hangchow man Yuan chattering at the gate. He scares me; I shall stay where I am." "And what is worse," he continued, "here's that Dr. Hsueh at the gate. He's a powerful practitioner. I must keep out of his way." Mr. Chiang was just pulling me aside so as to give the apparition room to pass, when Dr. Hsueh arrived. We told him at once what had been happening and he laughed heartily at what the ghost had said about being afraid of me and keeping out of Hsueh's way. "Take me to the patient", he said; and while I tidied up the room, Dr. Hsueh felt the young man's pulse. He gave him one dose of medicine, and he recovered. When the results were published, Chiang Pao-ch'en's name was thirty-eighth on the list.' Some years later, when Yuan Mei was again at Soochow, his cook suddenly began to have hallucinations, mistaking sunlight for snow, and so on. At the same time whenever he ate the least morsel he suffered from rending pains in the bowels. Several doctors treated him without success and finally Dr. Hsueh was again sent for. 'He stood with his hands folded in his sleeves gazing at the patient from top to toe, and after a while he said: "This is a cold cholera, one peeling will cure him". And sure enough a dark patch the size of a man's hand presently appeared on his body. It was scratched off, and he immediately recovered. When I expressed my astonishment and admiration, Dr. Hsueh said, "My doctoring is like your poetry. It is simply an operation of the spirit. Other men's art, as the saying goes, is a stay-at-home; mine comes from beyond the skies." '

This cook, Wang Hsiao-yü, was a remarkable man. 'When he first came', writes Yuan Mei, 'and asked what was to be the menu for the day, I feared that he had grand ideas, and I explained to him that I came of a family that was far from rich and that we were not in the habit of spending a fortune on every meal. "Very good", he said, laughing, and presently produced a plain vegetable soup which was so good that one went on and on taking it till one really felt one needed nothing more. . . . He insisted on doing all the marketing himself, saying, "I must see things in their natural state before I can decide whether I can apply my art to them". He never made more than six or seven dishes, and if more were asked for, he would not cook them. At the stove, he capered like a sparrow, but never took his eyes off it for a moment, and if when anything was coming to a boil someone called out to him, he took not the slightest notice, and did not even seem to hear. . . . When he said, "The soup is done", the kitchen-boy would rush up with the tureen and take it, and if by any chance the boy was slow, Wang would fly into a terrible rage and curse him roundly. . . . I once said to him, "If it were a question of your producing your results when provided with rare and costly ingredients, I could understand your achievements. What astonishes me is that, out of a couple of eggs, you can make a dish that no one else could have made." "The cook who can work only on a large scale must lack daintiness", he replied, "just as one who can handle common ingredients but fails with rare and costly ones can only be reckoned as a feeble practitioner. Good cooking, however, does not depend on whether the dish is large or small, expensive or economical. If one has the art, then a piece of celery or salted cabbage can be made into a marvellous delicacy; whereas if one has not the art, not all the greatest delicacies and rarities of land, sea or sky are of any avail . . . ." I once asked him why, when he could easily have got a job in some affluent household, he had preferred to stay all these years with me in the Sui Yuan. "To find an employer who appreciates one is not easy", he said. "But to find one who understands anything about cookery, is harder still. So much imagination and hard thinking go into the making of every dish that one may well say I serve up along with it my whole mind and heart. The ordinary hard-drinking revellers at a fashionable dinner-party would be equally happy to gulp down any stinking mess. They may say what a wonderful cook I am, but in the service of such people my art can only decline. True appreciation consists as much in detecting faults as in discovering merits. You, on the contrary, continually criticize me, abuse me, fly into a rage with me, but on every such occasion make me aware of some real defect; so that I would a thousand times rather listen to your bitter admonitions than to the sweetest praise. In your service, my art progresses day by day. Say no more! I mean to stay on here." But when he had been with me not quite ten years, he died; and now I never sit down to a meal without thinking of him and shedding a tear.'

It is time to return from the subject of his cook to that of his doctor. In Yuan Mei's own mind the two subjects were not wholly disconnected; for like many epicures he had a weak stomach, and though he was safe in his own cook's hands, he knew that much dining-out was bad for him. When his Manchu patron Yin-chi-shan returned to Nanking in 1751 and he knew that he would be constantly dining at his house, he addressed to Yin-chi-shan the poem:

I hear that again we shall have the ruler on whom our hearts were set;
All the worthies of Kiangnan are looking out their dress-clothes.
My wife looks forward to our own kitchen having an easy time;
My doctor fears that, so soon after my illness, I shall be difficult to treat.

When long afterwards (perhaps about 1775) Dr. Hsueh died at a great age, Yuan Mei intended to write an account of his life. He was dismayed to receive from the doctor's grandson an obituary in which the fact that he was a doctor was never mentioned at all. In the eyes of young Mr. Hsueh his grandfather's chief claim to fame was the fact that he had once taught philosophy to someone who afterwards became a Grand Secretary!

In the same year (1750) Yuan Mei himself was again taken ill at Soochow and was again cured by Dr. Hsueh, the treatment consisting merely in taking a decoction of quince (presumably quince leaves) instead of tea.

In 1751 the Emperor visited the southern provinces. Such Imperial Tours, though they served no doubt to keep up the interest of the nation in its sovereign, entailed enormous economic dislocation. Much of the grain usually sent to Peking had to be retained in the south, as the Emperor and Dowager Empress arrived with a horde of officials and attendants. It was difficult to estimate how much these human locusts would consume and constant adjustments and readjustments had to be made. In the decree announcing the tour, the Emperor had of course made the usual promise that the arrangements for his reception would be on a modest scale and would inflict no burden on his people. But local officials regarded this clause as a mere conventional formula, and were not willing to run the risk of being impeached for disloyalty. Triumphal arches had to be erected, the embankments of the Grand Canal had to be repaired or rebuilt in order to accommodate safely the vast crowds that would assemble to watch the Royal Barges pass, temporary palaces had to be erected all along the route. All this necessitated impounding vast numbers of peasants at a time of year when their labour was urgently needed in the fields. Prices, of course, leapt up, and we find the Treasury calmly anticipating inflation and minting extra currency, just as we do when a war begins. Nor was it only the Exchequer and the population at large that suffered. Influential individuals whose houses the Emperor signified his intention of visiting were often on such occasions reduced to beggary by the expense of entertaining him. The cortège reached Soochow, where Yuan Mei had been staying since the summer of last year, in the second month of 1751, and stayed there for five days. In common with a number of other distinguished literary men Yuan was called upon to compose a poem of welcome. It consisted of twenty-four lines so elaborately allusive and euphuistic that they defy and certainly would not repay translation. That it gave any pleasure to the poet to produce this assortment of far-fetched tropes and fulsome adulations it is hard to believe. But not to have inserted it in his Collected Poems would have been an act of disloyalty. In such matters he was very punctilious, and it duly figures in Volume Seven. The Governor-General of Kiangnan and Kiangsi at this time was a famous administrator called Huang T'ing-kuei (1691–1759). He was very unpopular, and one of the reasons for this was that he had ignored the Emperor's appeal for economy in making the preparations for the Southern Tour. Already in the summer of 1750 an old school-friend of Yuan Mei's called Ch'ien Ch'i had sent in a Memorial to the Throne complaining of this. The Emperor thought that the reports were exaggerated, but promised an enquiry. At about the time of the Emperor's visit Yuan, in his capacity as an 'official on sick leave', addressed to Huang T'ing-kuei a long and remarkable letter, in which he analyses the reasons for the Governor-General's unpopularity. 'It is commoner', he says, 'for high officials to criticize the Emperor than for humble ones to criticize such persons as a Governor-General, despite the fact that the Emperor can, if he chooses, treat criticism as an offence and punish his critic, whereas a Governor-General cannot. The reason why criticism of Emperors, dangerous though it is, does often occur, is that everyone will know why such a critic has got into trouble, and ambitious people hope in this way to bring themselves to general notice. A Governor-General can, of course, always trump up some other charge against a critic, and impeach him. But in that case no one knows the real reason for his impeachment, and he gets no credit for his independence and courage. You, however, who yourself risked so much in two instances must be distressed that no one has hitherto dared to criticize you. The two cases I refer to are, first, when the Emperor sent orders to you to exterminate a tribe on the western frontier, you sent the order back to Court without comment, and ignored it, and secondly, when Ortai was all-powerful in the State, you alone dared to oppose his policies. You have been here three years and hitherto "no feathers have flown"; but people at large are full of resentment against you. You have not impeached or banished any administrator, but the whole civil service is seething with discontent. You have shown no bias against the military; but the army is at loggerheads with you. You have neither accepted bribes from legal disputants nor sold honours; but your administration is for some reason regarded as corrupt. The secret of all this is that your system attracts worthless men and repels valuable ones. It enabled you to establish authority over wild border tribes, but it is out of place in China proper. . . . Nor do you realize that individuals differ no less than peoples. You pride yourself on not inflicting punishment on officials or ordering executions, but asserting yourself merely by speaking in a severe and solemn tone and striking imposing attitudes. You do not realize that there are people on whom no punishment and certainly no scolding has any effect; whereas there are others who will scorn to accept even praise and encouragement if they are not given in a courteous way; some who even for a thousand ounces of silver will not lift a finger, but whom a single word might make your slaves for life. Some whom the merest hint will reduce to abject shame; whereas the severest punishment would fail to make any impression on them. But you persist in treating everyone alike. In Kansu, dealing with swiftly-moving border tribes, you were obliged to keep yourself quickly and constantly informed. You used the military for this purpose, and the work was carried out not by officers but by common soldiers who knew that if their information turned out to be correct they would be rewarded and that if it was baseless they would not get into trouble. You now apply this method of tracking down offenders to the soft and easy-going inhabitants of South China and, needless to say, it does not work.

'When the Emperor made his tour in the South and labour was needed for building bridges and so on, the ordinary taxes were remitted. It therefore came as a surprise when a special levy on each household was instituted to pay for the preparations, particularly in view of the fact that, in the Mandate announcing the tour, the Emperor repeatedly expressed the desire that it should not be made burdensome to the people. You ignored this desire, believing that His Majesty did not mean what he said; acting in fact on the principle that "the sovereign expresses himself in set forms; his Ministers carry out his real intentions". You say that the people of the South are unstable and lacking in patriotism, and that what they need is a painful reminder of their duties. You forget that patriotism is a virtue that can only grow of itself and where it will; it cannot be produced by intimidation.'

Later in the letter Yuan Mei develops the theory that the Governor-General actually courts unpopularity, so that the Emperor may say, 'This man has no friends, he belongs to no party; all he thinks of is his duty to me'. This immense letter (of which I have summarized only part) ends with the words 'Death-penalty, death-penalty!', meaning 'If I must die for saying all this, then I am ready to die'.

So far from 'dying' it seems (as I shall show later) that as a result of this letter he got a trip at Government expense to the north-west—a part of China that he did not know at all and was anxious to see; for here had lain the centre of Chinese civilization at the time of her most glorious productions in art and poetry. He had never intended his retirement from office to be more than a short respite—a 'rest under the trees', and at about the time when he wrote this letter he applied for a fresh post. He was ordered to go first of all to report at Peking and then proceed to Si-an, the capital of Shensi, and take up an as yet unspecified post.

In the first days of 1752, in intense cold, he started by road for Peking. About to become an official for the second time he felt 'much as a remarried widow must feel on her wedding-day'. Driving through eastern Anhwei in his rickety carriage he was about as uncomfortable 'as a captive crayfish wriggling in its basket'. The few moments during which he halted at a cottage near Ch'u-chou and shook the snow from his garments were 'worth a thousand pounds'. In Shantung province the weather improved and he climbed the I-shan mountain, hoping to find at the top one of the six inscriptions in which Li Ssu, the Prime Minister of the First Emperor, recorded his sovereign's achievements. The monument was put up in 219 B.C. and had already been lost or destroyed about a thousand years before Yuan Mei's time. 'I could not see the king of Ch'in's inscription', he writes, 'nor the paulownias mentioned in *The Tribute of Yü*.' As the paulownias were supposed to have grown there in the third millennium B.C. it was not surprising that they had disappeared. At Tung-o, further north in Shantung, he was again archæologizing:

Some deserted tombs had inscriptions, and I frequently checked my horse;
The wine-booths had no walls; so I could not inscribe poems—

a rather comical example of the sort of mechanical antithesis so much admired in his day.

He reached Peking in the third month. Unknown figures poured in and out of well-remembered gates. In the parks and gardens where he had so often wandered with friends ten years before, the mango-bird seemed to be 'his only surviving acquaintance'. The warmest welcome that he received was at the house of Liu-pao (1686–1762), the Manchu grandee who had presided over the Third Degree examinations when Yuan passed in 1739. As has already been explained, a strong bond united examiners and the candidates when they passed;

the candidates were their scholastic children. But a more personal bond (Yuan Mei explains in his short biography of Liu-pao) united the candidate to the official in charge of the examinations; for whereas the actual examiners did not know the names of the candidates whom they passed, the presiding official removed the slips that hid these names and gave his approval to a person rather than to a set of papers. Liu-pao was a descendant of the imperial family of the Chin Tartar dynasty which ruled over north China from A.D. 1115 to 1234. His grandfather Asitan in the seventeenth century was famous as a translator from Chinese into Manchu, and the Manchu versions of the principal Confucian classics are due to him. Liu-pao himself took his Third Degree in 1721 under curious circumstances. The official in charge, a certain Li Fu (1675–1750), revived what was supposed to have been a T'ang dynasty method of examination, the general reputation of the candidates being taken more into consideration than their actual examination replies. When the results were announced the unsuccessful candidates (among whom was Liu-pao) organized an angry demonstration, holding up Li's carriage in the street and blocking up his gate with tiles and stones, so that he could not drive in. 'The Emperor K'ang Hsi disapproved of Li's methods and ordered Prince Yung to go through the papers of the unsuccessful candidates. He reported very favourably on Liu-pao's papers, and Liu-pao was in consequence given the Third Degree by special decree. In 1742, when Liu-pao was at the Board of Civil Office, the Emperor asked him to recommend officials suitable for special promotion. He proposed recommending Yuan Mei, who, however, wanted to be within reach of his parents and preferred a small provincial post in south China. Another old friend whom he met at Peking was the fatherly official Shih I-chih, who had tried so unsuccessfully to teach him Manchu ten years before. He records in the funerary inscription written when Shih died in 1763 that when they met again the old man (he was now seventy) said to him, 'I hear that you have been doing very well in your post at

Nanking, but that you do not "avoid the frivolity of Tu Mu" '. Tu Mu was a T'ang poet who was famous for the number and alluring beauty of his concubines and singing-girls.

Yuan was at Peking for only about three weeks. 'A man', he says, 'is not a man till he has visited old Ch'ang-an.' On his way west he passed through Lo-yang, a place almost equally full of historical associations. Chinese poets in former times so far from eschewing well-worn themes positively preferred them. No poet thought himself worthy of the name if, when passing a spot often celebrated by poets, he too did not try his hand. For a millennium and a half hundreds of poets had written verses of sombre meditation when passing the Pei-mang hills, the burial-place of Lo-yang in ancient times:

With high mounds the hill is thickly spread;
I give them a glance and drive swiftly by.
A poem is here, but I cannot bring myself to make it;
Too many poets have tried their hand before.

—an ingenious way of using the fact that the theme was too hackneyed to use. This did not, however, mean that he was in general averse to handling well-worn themes. He paid particular attention to the tombs of ancient celebrities, some of them very ancient and very shadowy indeed; as for example P'an Ku, the giant who (equipped with mallet and chisel) spent 18,000 years in fashioning the Universe, and Pien-ch'iao, the legendary founder of the art of healing. Of this last tomb it was said that, though in many cases resort to it achieved miraculous cures, any person who had ever exhibited jealousy was at once stabbed to death by the doctor's ghost. This was because Pien-ch'iao had himself been stabbed by a jealous rival. Needless to say he wrote more than one poem about Ma-wei, the place where the Emperor Ming Huang was forced by his soldiers to strangle his mistress, Yang Kuei-fei.

He knew hardly anyone at Si-an ('old Ch'ang-an', once

capital of the T'ang dynasty), but had one great patron. Strangely enough this was Huang T'ing-kuei, the Governor-General to whom he had addressed the long letter of remonstrance. At the end of the year 1751 Huang had been transferred from the south and made Governor-General of Shensi and Kansu. It is evident from more than one passage in the poems of 1752, but particularly from the poem called 'Seeing off Huang, Guardian of the Heir Apparent, when he went on a tour of the frontier', that Yuan Mei now regarded himself as Huang's client and, in some sense, his official panegyrist; for the poem ends with a promise that in the ninth month, when Huang returns from his martial exploits, he will find Yuan Mei waiting for him 'with wet brush', ready to celebrate his achievements. It seems extremely likely that Yuan was allotted a post in Shensi because Huang T'ing-kuei, impressed by Yuan's letter, had specially asked for him. He may well have felt that someone who showed such an understanding of popular feelings and prejudices, and at the same time such a penetrating knowledge of his own character, would be useful as a subordinate. It would seem indeed that he escorted Huang to a considerable distance towards the frontier; for he has a poem about the historical associations of Ling-wu, the place where, after the abdication of Ming Huang in 756, his son was enthroned as Emperor of T'ang. It is most unlikely that he would have written such a poem if he had not actually accompanied his patron to the frontier. He also wrote a 'Frontier Song'; but many poets did that, on conventional lines, without ever having set foot outside central China. The heat at Ch'ang-an (i.e. Si-an) was intolerable:

In southern China in the hottest weather, one can still sleep at night;
But here in the west in hot weather one grills all night . . .
I have not yet made my move and am living in a small house;
It is like being walled with red embers at the bottom of a cooking-pot.

I have tried using a large fan, till my arms fell to my side;
But the wind it made was flaming hot and laden with yellow sand.
I thought of going into the outskirts to get away from the heat;
But the Serpentine exists no more and the K'un-ming is dry. . . .
On the Southern Hills tall there stands the Rain Making Altar—
A high official is to conduct the prayers, the double torches glow;
Behind his carriage and in front of his carriage monks and Taoists follow.
The 'rainbow-flags' and 'fire-umbrellas' make a fearful din;
The onlookers shake off their sweat, it pours down like rain. . . .
I am an official without a post, but also have my instructions:
'Fourth Watch at the yamen *gate; fifth watch at the shrine.'*
'What's it all to do with you?', the drought-demon asks;
And the clay-dragons titter at me for rushing about in the heat.
Suddenly my thoughts turn to the south, and my ten acres of mulberry;
I am pillowed high at my northern window where the cool wind blows.
What I am doing here in the heat I cannot understand—
I have found nothing but scorched earth and the memories of ancient kings.

The 'rainbow-flags' and 'fire-umbrellas', it should be explained, were names of two kinds of fireworks. Clay figures of rain-dragons were used in the rain-making ceremony.

In the autumn, when he had held an official post of some kind (we never learn what it was) for only three days, came the news that his father, after travelling in intense heat during the sixth month from Hangchow to Nanking, had died there early in the seventh month. Officials who were in mourning normally retired from their posts. Yuan Mei hurried straight back to Nanking, arriving there early in the winter.

CHAPTER FIVE

The Sui-pi *and the Ghost Stories*

WE know about the circumstances under which he returned to Nanking from a poem he wrote in answer to a letter of condolence from his friend Chuang Yu-kung, who had sat with him in the examination for the Third Degree and had secured the top place. During this year (1753) Chuang got into trouble under curious circumstances. As the accident was one which might equally well have befallen Yuan Mei himself, and as it illustrates the atmosphere of oppression and inquisition under which the subjects of the great Ch'ien Lung lived, the story is worth telling. In 1749 Chuang Yu-kung was acting as Examiner at Sung-chiang in Kiangsu. Someone pressed into his hand a number of books. Turning over rapidly a few pages, he encountered several times the expression 'The Philosopher Ting says. . . . ' He accepted the books, and when he got home made enquiries as to what sort of person this was who dignified himself with the title 'The Philosopher Ting'. He was told that the man was insane, and threw the books away, without making any further attempt to read them. Four years later the Governor of Shantung reported to the Throne that a man from Sung-chiang named Ting had presented him with some books which, on inspection, proved to be full of incitements to rebellion against the Manchus. The Governor asked that the case should be dealt with speedily, as Ting was in a bad way mentally and physically, and was unlikely to survive a long period of detention in gaol. The Emperor replied that Chuang Yu-kung had shown gross neglect of his duty in not examining the contents of the books, and the Governor impertinence in demanding that any consideration should be shown to a criminal who was circulating anti-Manchu literature. A deduction of one-tenth was made from Chuang's salary as Commissioner for Education in Kiangsu. The wretched Philosopher Ting was presumably executed. This mishap of Chuang Yu-kung's might, as I have said, easily have befallen Yuan Mei himself. If a lunatic had pressed a book into his hands, we cannot imagine his doing otherwise than accept it courteously and then, as—contrary to what one might expect—books by lunatics usually make very tame reading, throw it away unread.

Of all the various kinds of 'witch-hunting' that went on during Ch'ien Lung's reign, it was obviously the Literary Inquisition that touched Yuan most nearly. He was not likely to be accused of belonging to one of the secret resistance associations, such as the 'Iron-footrule Club', which were constantly being routed out and exterminated. But he continually ran the risk of, for example, writing a preface to the work of some friend and then discovering that it contained some turn of phrase capable of being interpreted as disrespectful to the reigning dynasty; or of including in an anthology (and he was the maker of a number of anthologies) a poem by someone who in some other work, unknown to the anthologist, had exalted racial patriotism or mentioned without opprobrium one of the Ming princes who carried on opposition to the Manchus after the fall of the Ming dynasty. Nor indeed was it the Chinese only who ran these risks; Yuan Mei's Manchu friends also suffered. In this same year (1753) all translations into Manchu of what was regarded as frivolous literature had to be surrendered by their owners, and even all versions in which the Chinese text (for the convenience of Manchus who could not read the Chinese characters) was spelt out in Manchu writing. One of the books specifically mentioned was the *Shui Hu Chuan*, well known to Western readers in Pearl Buck's translation (*All*

Men are Brothers). This, a tale of the Robin Hood type, was perhaps partly banned because it might tend to promote the view that an oppressed people were justified in taking matters into their own hands. Naturally, too, European books aroused suspicion. In the sixth month of this year the Governor of Hupeh announced that some works in foreign writing, including a medical text, had fallen into his hands. As neither he nor any of his colleagues could read them he proposed to send them to Peking, to be translated by the Catholic missionaries employed at the Imperial Observatory. The Emperor replied that the missionaries at Peking would, if the books were traitorous, certainly not involve their colleagues in trouble by revealing the fact. No one else at Peking could read Western Ocean languages, and the case had better be dealt with on the spot. But it was the Emperor's opinion that the missionaries were in general peaceable and law-abiding people, and he did not think it likely that they would be found to be connected with any seditious movement. Yuan Mei though, as has been mentioned, he knew a Christian Manchu prince, does not seem to have had any contact with Missionaries either at Peking or in the provinces. There was, till 1774, a theoretical Bishopric at Nanking, but the bishops were only able to pay occasional *sub-rosa* visits to the city, and for the most part spent their time going from village to village, ministering to small groups of secret converts.

It must not then be thought that, in escaping from the notorious perils of public life, Yuan Mei in his garden had ensconced himself in an atmosphere of calm and security. More than at any previous time in Chinese history the writer of books of any kind was under suspicion. Quite apart from the question of orthodox political views there was that of philosophical orthodoxy. The whole educational and examination system was based on the Neo-Confucian interpretation of the Classics, and any criticism of this interpretation could be made a case for impeachment (*k'o*). In 1729, for example, the scholar Hsieh Chi-shih was impeached (though unsuccessfully) by a Manchu General for making a commentary on the *Great Learning* in which he attacked the orthodox Neo-Confucian commentaries. But later in the century the attention of the Government became more and more riveted on suppressing anti-Manchu literature, and the attitude towards unorthodox scholarship became laxer. This was inevitable; for during the second half of the eighteenth century the orthodox interpretation of the Classics began to be discarded by all serious scholars, and survived merely as an instrument of mass education. True, even towards the end of the century the great bibliographer Chi Yun (1724–1805) when accusing the Neo-Confucians of devoting all their attention to Heaven, Nature, the Mind and other such shadowy entities, instead of to practical problems, still took the precaution of putting these criticisms into the mouth of a ghost. But I suspect that he was merely parodying the grotesque precautions taken by unorthodox scholars of a previous generation.

Yuan Mei, following the general tendency of his time, freely criticized (particularly towards the end of his life) both the general views and the scholarship of the Neo-Confucians; but there is, I think, no evidence that he ever got into trouble for doing so.

He does not seem to have taken the obligations of mourning very seriously. Towards the turn of the year (1752–1753) we find him giving a wine-party, after which his friend the calligrapher T'ao Yung wrote on his door-screen the account of the Sui-yuan garden (and how he came to purchase it) which had been composed by Yuan in the spring of 1749. While the calligrapher was at work, his eyes met those of a servant-girl called A-chao. He took a great fancy to her, but was too shy to say so, and only betrayed his feelings by the fact that he treated her with exaggerated respect and that he put an unwonted zest and verve into his calligraphy. The tutor Lü Wen-kuang (the one who, it will be remembered, had forged an examination essay) acted as go-between, and on the seventh day of the New Year, amid scenes of general festivity, T'ao formally took the girl as his concubine.

Some weeks later Yuan married Lü Wen-kuang to his wife's younger sister and wrote a bridal poem in which he sagely warned him that the seeds of virtue which his deep studies had implanted would now be expected by the family to bear fruit. To this time belongs one of the rather rare references to his brother Yuan Chien, who was some years older than his favourite brother Yuan Shu and was now serving as Prefect in a district near Nanking: 'My brother grows orchids, and a tame deer broke loose and ate all the leaves. My brother was angry and sentenced the deer to imprisonment. When I heard of this I wrote a note begging for its release, but had no one by whom to send it. Happily the Bachelor Ho Hsi-fang of Hangchow came to see me and gladly undertook to deliver it. On the evening of the day that the note arrived four bowmen appeared carrying a police-litter. On being released, the deer dashed off with such rapidity that I got no near view of it. Soon, however, it reappeared, high up on the hill-side, and in among the trees, crying, kicking its heels, and making obeisances with its head, with all the air of a condemned criminal who has been reprieved, content with its new abode as the poet Li Po when he escaped the death-penalty and was sent to Yeh-lang, or Su Tung-p'o when he was set at large in the island of Hai-nan. I therefore sent a poem to my brother thanking him on the creature's behalf for its reprieve and on my own for this present of a deer.'

To this period, too, belongs a charming poem about a picture called 'Returning Boat', painted for him by his friend Ni Su-feng:

I had long had it in mind to make a boat
That should skim the waves quick as any bird
Yet never carry people away from their friends,
But only carry people back to their homes.
Its misty sails and bamboo paddles existed only as a dream;
Year after year, a traveller afar, I was plagued by winds and sands.

Su-feng, brush in hand, looked at me and laughed,
Then bending over his painting-paper he chortled to himself.
What before was only a dream has today become a picture;
Now I really have *come home; suddenly I realize it!*

Yuan Mei wrote poetry in two sharply contrasted styles. There were the intimate, generally humorous poems that he wrote for his friends, and the formal, solemn poems that he addressed to important acquaintances, particularly to high military officers. Of the latter kind is a series of poems addressed to General Wu Shih-sheng, whom he met this year (1753) at a tavern in the gay quarter of Nanking. The general told him how during the campaign against the Golden River aborigines, when one of the chieftains expressed a desire to surrender, he (General Wu) had asked the Commander-in-Chief to let him go and accept the surrender. He had ridden all alone to the chieftain's tent and, as it was late, had at once asked for a pillow, upon which he slept soundly till day-light. He had then gathered the chieftains and sub-chieftains round him and harangued them upon their iniquity in rebelling against the Emperor. 'They had not a word to say for themselves', the General recounted. 'Presently they killed an ox and roasted it, and then gave a big show of some of their barbarous dances. After that we drew up the treaty.'

As became a gay, peaceable southerner, Yuan Mei had an awed appreciation of bluff, soldierly tales. He took an unquestioning pride in Ch'ien Lung's far-flung conquests, wrote accounts of several generals and their exploits, and addressed (as I have said) a number of poems to important military men. There was indeed, to varying degrees, a certain strain of pacifism in each of China's 'Three Religions'. Some Buddhists were out-and-out pacifists; as for example, the seventh-century pilgrim Hsuan-tsang ('Tripitaka'), who refused to accompany the Emperor T'ai-tsung on his Manchurian campaign in 746. Taoists, basing their attitude on a famous passage in the *Tao Te Ching*, countenanced war only 'as a last resort'. Confucians, on the whole, believed that only those wars were justified which had as their aim 'to punish evil-doers'. But as anyone, 'anywhere under Heaven', who did not accept the Chinese Emperor as overlord was accounted as an 'evil-doer' Confucian pacifism did not really amount to anything. There was, so far as I know, no real political opposition to Ch'ien Lung's wars of conquest in Turkestan, Tibet, Burma, etc. Being carried on chiefly by Manchu troops, they did not immediately affect the Chinese, except in the matter of increased taxation.

In the autumn of 1753 Yuan Mei wrote a second account of his garden. On returning from Shensi at the end of 1752 he found both the garden itself and the pavilions in a state of hopeless devastation and disrepair. Some of his friends told him that for the money he would have to spend to put all this to rights he could buy a fine house and garden in perfect condition. He replied that not even the most spacious mansion, replete with historical and literary associations, would interest him at all, 'because there would be nothing of myself in it'. Nor would it interest him, even if he could afford it, to hire hordes of workmen to produce a ready-made estate in a specified time, taking no part in the work himself and merely receiving congratulations when it was finished. The rich people who can afford to do this, he says, generally do not even know the names of the trees that have been planted. 'The work on my garden may never be finished, my expenditure on it may well prove beyond my means. Very well then; some things that are lacking will have to wait till they can be supplied; some things that are broken will have to wait till they can be repaired. There is no fixed time by which anything has to be done. Whatever happens I shall be better off than in old days when I had to be all the time bowing and scraping to jacks-in-office. I can get rid of a weed or lop off a twisted bough on my own initiative, without anyone directing me and "impeding my elbow".

'I am just thirty-seven. I am determined to settle here.

Whether I can make something of this place and live in it permanently only the future can decide.'

On the eleventh day of the seventh month the plans for making the garden habitable received a sad check owing to the death of Yuan's carpenter, Wu Lung-t'ai. 'He was very tall, spare, and immensely strong. All the pavilions and arbours in my garden were his work. He had no family, so I took charge of his funeral and buried him in a western corner of the garden, addressing this poem to his spirit:

Life has a pattern, has its retributions;
Such things cannot be mere chance.
It fell to you to make my house;
It fell to me to make your coffin.
I buried you in a corner of the garden,
And having done so, felt at peace with myself,
For I felt as though you still came and went
Among the things your own hand had made.
A fresh wind fans your mortal form;
The wild wheat makes you its offerings—
Happier here than if pious sons and grandsons
Had carried you off to the dismal fringes of the town.
Here forever you shall be our Guardian Spirit,
Unsaddened by the murky winds of Death.

Perhaps from about the same time dates the account of the dwarf Chao Yuan-wen. 'At the age of 27 he was about two feet high. He had a broad face and huge lips. His head was like an inverted cauldron. When he walked he wobbled from side to side, and if he stood for long, his buttocks pressed on to the back of his knees. His fingers were clenched in a ball and he could not straighten them. A Mr. Ching Shou-pei of Yangchow gave this dwarf's mother a thousand cash (about 6s.), and took the dwarf to live with him. He taught him to receive guests correctly. The dwarf had his wits about him, and though there was not much that he could do, he could bow a little, by bending one knee, and whenever a guest arrived at the house he at once sidled to the door and put his bow into practice. Cheng presently succeeded in finding a girl-dwarf of just the same height and wanted to pair them off. But the man-dwarf would not hear of it. "We dwarfs", he said, "are poor folk whom Heaven has made for derision. I have a mother, but cannot work to support her. I have no desire on top of that to have a woman-dwarf to look after." Cheng tried to insist, but the dwarf threatened to leave him, and in the end Cheng gave way. When I was at Yangchow I went to stay with Cheng and on my arrival the dwarf came out, bowed to me, and enquired after my health. While I was there he came every morning and every evening, and saluted me. I took him back with me to Nanking, where everyone from generals and governors downward, hearing how minute he was, vied with one another in asking him to their houses and entertaining him. Again and again he brushed the earth with his knee, then raised his head and made civil speeches, his whole manner most deferential, ingratiating and accommodating. Everyone was delighted with him, he received countless presents, and returned to Yangchow, his boxes laden with flowing cloaks and large hats.'

The phraseology of this little essay (a fact not possible to make apparent in translation) throws an interesting light on Yuan Mei's methods of composition. It is evident that before writing it he looked up the section on Court Jesters (many of whom were dwarfs) in the *Shih Chi*, the earliest Chinese history, and to give his essay a proper 'dwarf' colouring, borrowed some archaic phrases from it. But while he was doing so a couple of phrases in the next section of the *Shih Chi* (which has nothing to do with dwarfs) caught his eye, and he worked in these two phrases as well.

The Chinese were quite used to dwarfs who, as in Europe, had played the role of jesters and playthings in the mansions of the great since very early times. But a dwarf only two feet high (and the 'foot' intended did not differ greatly from the English foot) is a great rarity, and I think it was his extreme smallness (coupled with his good manners) that made this dwarf such a success.

In 1754 on the walls of a monastery at Yangchow (about fifty miles north-west of Nanking) Yuan Mei found a much effaced poem, which he greatly admired. It was signed 'T'iao-sheng', which was obviously a 'courtesy name' (*tzu*), not an official name (*ming*). Anyone could have been called T'iao-sheng, and though he violently desired to get into touch with the poet, it was impossible to do so unless he knew his real name and surname. He copied out the poem and rushed out into the street with it, asking everyone he met who T'iao-sheng was. 'I asked and asked till my lips were dry and my tongue parched; but no one could tell me.' At last a fellow Academician called Chang Ti-chai, with whom he was having a drink, was able, when the name T'iao-sheng was mentioned, at once to tell him that this was the courtesy name of a young man called Chiang Shih-ch'üan, who was now at Peking, trying to get his Third Degree.

Chiang Shih-ch'üan (1725–1785) is the best-known dramatist of the eighteenth century. He was also a considerable poet; his name is often coupled with that of Yuan Mei and the two poets produced a joint anthology of their poems. He had, by 1754, already written six plays, probably to the detriment of his examination studies. Having found out Chiang's address at Peking, Yuan Mei wrote to him and found to his delight that the young man knew and admired his poems. A correspondence ensued, and continued year after year, 'without my ever knowing whether he was tall or short, lean or fat'. It was not, I think, till 1764 that they actually met; but Chiang, he tells us, sent him 'a great many plays'. Of Chiang's plays, only nine are now easily accessible; one or two others are said to exist in rare first editions. He seems to have written with great rapidity. In 1751 alone, when he was 26, he wrote four plays. In 1769 he wrote *The Evergreen Tree* (consisting of thirty-eight episodes) in three days, and wrote two other plays in the same year. An 'episode' was much longer than the average 'scene' in Western plays, though generally rather shorter than an 'act'. Probably his best-known play is *Four Strings at Autumn*, written in 1772. The fourth episode, 'Seeing off a Guest', is still sometimes performed. It is a dramatization of the T'ang poet Po Chü-i's *Lute Girl's Song*. Previous plays on the subject, says Chiang in his preface, had shown a laughable ignorance about the true facts of Po Chü-i's life. He, for his part, has stuck to the facts and to the text of the 'Song'. Each of the four episodes has indeed as its title a couplet from the *Lute Girl's Song*. The meagre concrete data of the Song are expanded by somewhat pedantic methods. For example, at the beginning of the play the Lute Girl's husband (a tea merchant) and his associate each give a full catalogue of the different kinds of tea they have bought in a dozen different places, along with the exact quantities. I personally prefer the method of earlier playwrights who, far closer to the people, expanded their themes by weaving into them popular legends and mythology. (The play, it may be mentioned in parenthesis, was written at the suggestion of some friends with whom in the late autumn of 1772 Chiang Shih-ch'üan discussed previous plays on the subject. It is interesting that one of these friends was Yuan Mei's brother, Yuan Chien.) Most of Chiang's plays are indeed dramatized chronicles rather than dramas, and one of them, *The Dream of Lin-ch'uan*, is a detailed biography, in twenty episodes, of an earlier dramatist, T'ang Hsien-tsu (1550–1617). At the same time there is, at any rate in the nine accessible plays, always a strong element of the supernatural—of earthly characters who are really banished Immortals, of heavenly warnings, prophetic dreams, of Taoist magic and in general of a spiritual world at every turn impinging upon the world of common reality. Nor were these elements, I think, introduced merely as dramatic conventions. This half-hidden but ever-present world, a compound of Buddhist and Taoist belief and of native folklore, and all its happenings were as real to almost everyone in eighteenth-century China as the events of everyday life. Some modern Chinese critics have labelled Chiang Shih-ch'üan a 'realist'. But this is only true if we take it to mean (which is not at all what the critics had in mind) that in his dramas he showed life in all its facets, natural and supernatural, as he really believed it to be.

Some of the plays, we know, were written for special local occasions and performed on the spot. It may well be that others were never acted at all. That they could be regarded as novels in dramatic form and read as such with avidity is shown by a passage in the *Play Tales* of Li T'iao-yuan (1734–1803) in which he tells how when he passed through Nan-ch'ang (in about 1782), hoping to meet Chiang, he found that the dramatist was at Peking; but Chiang's son gave him several of the plays to read, including *The Evergreen Tree* and *The Man in the Snow*. He became so absorbed in the plays that he had travelled several hundred leagues without being conscious that the scene had changed at all; and even found that he had passed the terrifying Eighteen Rapids of the Kan River, on his way to Canton, without ever noticing them!

Yuan Mei himself certainly never had a similar experience. He tells us in Chapter XV of his *Poetry Talks* that in plays, considered as reading matter, he took no interest. 'Chiang Shih-ch'üan', he says, 'once forced me to read one of his plays, saying, "You must take into account that play-writing is my special infirmity. Please do me the kindness of having a look at it". Seeing there was no way out, I looked through several episodes. Next day he came and asked if anything in it had pleased me. "Yes," I said, "there are two lines that I like:

> *Clever though you are, yet shall you never guess*
> *What Heaven has in mind.*"

He laughed and said, "One sees that you are a poet not a playwright".'

Chiang then showed that the couplet was based on one by Shang P'an (1701–1767). But in saying 'you are a poet not a playwright' Chiang Shih-ch'üan was also, I think, referring to the fact that in quoting the lines Yuan Mei had translated them out of the special language used in dramatic lyrics into that of ordinary poetry. The quotation is from episode 16 of the play *Perfume in an Empty Valley*.

In 1754 the Manchu grandee Yin-chi-shan had his headquarters at Huai-an, where he was in charge of a River Conservancy job. From here he sent a messenger to Yuan Mei with a letter summoning him to take a post at Huai-an, a plea that their mutual friend Shen Feng, the painter and calligrapher (1695–1757) was ordered to support with 'the strongest recommendations and remonstrances'. We do not possess Yin-chi-shan's letter, but Yuan's reply to it is in Vol. 19 of his Prose Works. In it he says: 'I know what is in your mind. During the forty years that you have served at Court and in the provinces you have behaved with punctilious discretion, and never once got into trouble. . . . But I am known to be so closely bound to you as friend and disciple that our fates are linked. If I came a cropper, you would at once be involved; so that these warnings to me are made in your own interest rather than in mine.'

It is worth noting that in the Manchu dynasty penal code (Ch. XXXIII) there is a clause: 'All officials, civil or military, who spend the night at the residence of a prostitute or who bring singing-girls to drink with them are liable to sixty blows of the rod.' A prostitute (*ch'ang*) is defined as meaning any woman (whether registered as a musician or not) who lived by prostitution. A singing-girl (*chi*) meant, I suppose, a woman registered as a 'musician', not as an ordinary free citizen. This clause, though in general it was ignored, could always be invoked against anyone of particularly scandalous life. That Yuan Mei had a reputation for loose living we have already seen above (p. 60), and further evidence will be brought. The phrase 'come a cropper', which I have translated literally, presumably refers to the possibility that Yuan's amours might eventually land him in disaster. It is certain that in his later years Yuan Mei ceased to take any interest in singing-girls. There is a famous ironic letter refusing an invitation to a geisha-party, and round about

1790 he writes in his *Poetry Talks*: 'After I reached middle age I ceased to take any pleasure in geisha-parties. People thought I had been converted to strict Confucianism; they did not realize that if one is to "look at flowers" they must be "flowers" that take one's fancy.'

It is of course possible that Yin-chi-shan's letter refers to some other form of indiscretion; for example to Yuan's cult of boy-actors. Or again, he may have been running after some respectable person's wife or unmarried daughter; but there is no evidence of this.

At the end of the third month he went to Huai-an, not to accept the post, but to make it clear that his decision to remain a free man was final: 'I have retired forever to my garden and have long given up all thoughts of the dusty world. You not only summoned me by letter but told Shen Feng to support your plea with the strongest recommendations and remonstrances. You are like the fond mother of Tseng Ts'an, who believed in false rumours about her own son; you are like the hasty doctor who prescribes before he has taken the patient's pulse. Evidently your fears about me and your love of me are far from being matched by an equal knowledge of my real character. To speak my mind frankly, I prefer to imitate K'ung Sung.'

When three different people had repeated to Tseng Ts'an's mother the false rumour that her son, a pupil of Confucius, had committed a murder, she at last believed in the unbelievable, threw down her shuttle and fled. K'ung Sung was a worthy of Han times who preferred working as a hired labourer to taking a post in the Civil Service. A friend who had become Governor of the district thought K'ung must feel his present position to be humiliating, and offered him a job. 'Poverty is the common lot of scholars', said K'ung Sung. 'Why should I feel humiliated?' And he went on working as a hired labourer.

It is clear from the first allusion (as also from Yin-chi-shan's letter) that the 'false rumours' he had heard were not merely reports that Yuan Mei wanted to return to public office. They must certainly have been rumours that imputed to him reprehensible behaviour of some kind. There was, as we shall see, similar trouble on two subsequent occasions; indeed, in 1772 he was on the verge of being banished from Nanking. What these rumours were, and whether they were of the same kind on each of the three occasions we have no means of deciding. The only document that throws any light on the subject is a mock 'deposition' about Yuan's conduct alleged to have been written by his friend the poet Chao I (1727–1814). It is couched in a facetious parody of legal language, and would be very difficult to translate in full. One of the charges is that Yuan, having settled in his garden, 'ransacked the neighbourhood for whatever was soft and warm, not minding whether it was boy or girl'. 'He entices young ladies of good family to his house,' the document goes on, 'and all the "moth-eyebrows" (i.e. handsome girls) are enlisted as his pupils.' 'He regards himself as stage-manager of all the elegances; but is in reality a sinner against the teachings of Confucius.' The plaintiff ends by demanding that the miscreant should forthwith be executed and then, if his crimes seem to demand it, reincarnated as a bee or butterfly, as penalty for his frivolities in this life; or if a lighter view is taken, 'should be returned to his former lair, there to lead as before a robust existence, chasing the apes on his hill'. The plaint is evidently made to the Jade Emperor in Heaven rather than to the earthly authorities. But fanciful and jocular though it is, I think it gives us a fair idea of the complaints against Yuan that were made by straight-laced people. The great cause of scandal, at any rate towards the latter part of his life, was probably his 'moth-eyebrow' academy. Many people, though by no means all, disapproved of women receiving a literary education, and others no doubt felt that if a woman took lessons in poetry and so on, it should be in her home, and not at the house of a 'gay genius', known to be far from strict in his views.

Probably no man in China ever had more friends than Yuan Mei. But no one who wielded so caustic a pen could fail also to have enemies; moreover from many stories that he tells about himself it is clear that he had a hasty temper. Some of the attacks on him may therefore have been due to resentment and personal hostility rather than to moral disapprobation.

The year 1754 ended badly, with the death of several friends and relations, and finally with one of the worst bouts of malaria that Yuan Mei ever had, lasting from the eighth month till the end of the year. On New Year's Eve when he was 'only distant by the space of one lamp from next year', when on his body 'frail as the banana-leaf', 'through cracks in the wall the wind darted like an assassin'—he sat listening to the cloud-shattering reports of his neighbours' crackers and mixing the ink for the writing of the last poem of his thirty-ninth year.

In 1755 he received a letter from an old friend called Ch'eng T'ing-tso, with whom he had sat for the special examination at Peking in 1736 and who had then, owing to his girlish beauty, been nicknamed 'Miss Ch'eng'. In this letter Ch'eng urged him to read the *Śūrangama Sūtra*, a Buddhist work that had, for about a thousand years, enjoyed immense popularity in China. I will first of all explain what this book is about, and then go on to say something about Ch'eng T'ing-tso (1691–1767) and about Yuan Mei's general attitude towards Buddhism.

The *Śūrangama*, which purports to be an ancient Indian text translated from Sanskrit, is in fact, as all Buddhist scholars now agree, a treatise composed in Chinese by some Chinese monk at the beginning of the eighth century A.D. It begins with a story about Buddha's devoted but wayward disciple Ānanda, whose spiritual career was handicapped by his great personal beauty. One day when he was going round with his begging-bowl a courtesan-sorceress of the Mātanga clan, which specialized in spells and magic, saw him pass and fell deeply in love with him. She laid the inherited family spell upon him and he was just on the point of disgracing his Order by yielding to her charms (using the word in both its senses) when Buddha became aware of what was happening and in the nick of time used an even more powerful counter-charm and rescued him from her embraces. Buddha then explained to Ānanda that all emotional impressions come through the senses and that the first essential, for anyone wishing to combat the devastating assaults of the senses, is to know where they are located. 'It is like when a country is infested by bandits. The king of the country tells his soldiers to attack them, but how can the soldiers do this, if they do not know where the bandits are?' A long discussion follows in which it is proved that the sense of sight cannot be located in the eye, nor the sense of smell in the nose, and so on. Nor can it be located either in the thing seen or in the contact between eye and thing. The upshot of the argument (too long and complicated to study here) is that all sense-perceptions are misinterpretations of an undifferentiated, unconditioned, transcendental state of affairs. If Ānanda could but learn to 'enter deeply' into this Absolute, he would have no more trouble with his 'six senses'. The object of the book then is not merely to gratify philosophic curiosity by exploring a difficult problem. The king does not send out his spies merely to find out who and where the bandits are, and leave it at that. If he takes steps to locate them, it is with a view to bringing them to their knees. One may then call the book an essay in 'applied epistemology', just as one talks of 'applied anthropology', in cases where the anthropologist studies primitive people in order to be better able to rule them.

Ch'eng T'ing-tso, who wanted Yuan Mei to read this book, was in his earlier days a follower of one of the schools that rejected the semi-Buddhist metaphysics of the Neo-Confucians, and he refused to see in the Classics anything but a discussion of concrete, human affairs. But later in life, perhaps out of prudence (for attacks on Chu Hsi were still punishable) and perhaps partly out of disgust at the indiscriminate violence with which disagreement with Sung philosophers was currently expressed, he ceased to speak or write against them, except when addressing a few intimate friends. An odder reason may also have been at work. He was greatly distressed at having no son to carry on the ancestral sacrifices after his death, and his teacher, the great Confucian Fang Pao (1668–1749), had written a whole treatise, accompanied by unconvincing statistics, to prove that people who attacked the Neo-Confucians seldom produced sons. It may be that it was in the hope of inducing Heaven to give him an heir that he ceased to attack the Neo-Confucians openly.

In 1754 Ch'eng had a severe illness and nearly died. It was perhaps during this illness that he took to reading the *Śūrangama*; at any rate it was during the next year that he recommended the book (which surely is at any rate worth reading) to Yuan Mei. Yuan replied that the work was a forgery of the Six Dynasties period (third to sixth centuries A.D.) and that 'speaking broadly' it contained nothing that was not to be found in the discourses of the Sung philosophers (eleventh to thirteenth centuries A.D.). He was right about it being a forgery, but dated it many centuries too early. The suggestion that it contained nothing that was not also in Neo-Confucian dialogues is absurd. It is indeed apparent from a letter written about 1779 to a friend called Hsiang Yung, with whom he often stayed at Hangchow, that he had scarcely done more than glance at the book. 'When I was 39', he wrote, 'my old friend Ch'eng T'ing-tso suddenly urged me to read the *Śūrangama Sūtra*. He said he regarded me as extremely intelligent and was sure that, if I would only read the book, I should take to it at once. I followed his advice, but alas before I had finished a chapter I found myself yawning and stretching, and thinking of bed. What he found striking, I found commonplace; what to him seemed profound, to me seemed muddled. The explanation can only be that our natures are different. I suppose I have inherited no incense-burning *karma* from my previous existence. Of course this word *karma* is itself derived from Buddhism. But one has only to look about the world around one to be absolutely convinced that such a thing does operate, and I regard this theory of reincarnation as filling a gap in the teaching of our native sages. So you see I am quite open-minded. I am ready to accept a truth wherever it comes from, without being tied down to all the views either of Confucians or Buddhists.' The book, it should be observed, consists of ten chapters; so Yuan did not get very far. The sort of evidence that he alludes to was, for example, the fact that all over China (as of course in India too) people were constantly cropping up who remembered their previous existence and could recount it in detail. His chief objection to Buddhism was that it regarded every kind of sensuous or sensual gratification as immoral. This, of course, could not be reconciled with Yuan Mei's view that one should enjoy without misgiving whatever good things Nature gave us to enjoy. But he knew extremely little about Buddhism. Indeed, as he explains in the letter just quoted, he never found the day long enough to get through all the reading he wanted to do simply in order to have a complete knowledge of the Histories and Classics. How could he possibly have any time or strength left to devote to other, alien studies?

Several of Yuan Mei's friends were believers in Buddhism and one of them, P'eng Shao-sheng (1740–1796), devoted the greater part of his life to writing Buddhist propaganda. 'He was brought up', writes Yuan Mei, 'in surroundings of great elegance and luxury, but became a fervent believer in Zen Buddhism, and from his middle years onwards was a strict vegetarian. He and his wife lived under separate roofs. Twice a month, on the first and fifteenth days, he would look in and say, "I hope you are not forgetting your devotions". Apart from that they never set eyes on each other. Later on he shut himself up in a hut near the Western Lake at Hangchow. But happily, during all this time, he never gave up writing poetry.'

P'eng, of course, tried to convert Yuan Mei. 'Surely', he wrote, 'where we came from when we were born and where we shall go to when we die are questions of the utmost importance and cannot be simply ignored.' 'I think they can', answered Yuan Mei. 'Not knowing where we came from when we were born does not prevent us from being born, and not knowing where we go to when we die does not make us die a moment the sooner.' 'You misunderstand me', replied P'eng. 'I was not referring to the sequence of birth and death, but to the conceptions "birth" and "death" as held by us at any one moment. Our belief that such things exist at all is due to an accumulation of momentary conceptions. "Finishing with birth and death" does not involve an assertion that we were never born and that we shall never die.' 'In your first letter', replied Yuan, 'you were plainly talking about the birth and death of the individual. But in your second you change round, and say that you meant the conception of birth and death as held by us at any one moment. . . . You go on to say that this conception is due to the pursuit of sensual pleasures. But what makes a live man different from a dead one is precisely that he is capable of enjoying such pleasures.' 'What you are asking me to do', Yuan Mei continues, 'is to behave as though I were dead, when in fact I am not dead. Can there be any sense in this?'

At one point in the first letter Yuan Mei, abandoning argument, makes the assertion that 'all these tales about Buddha are mere senseless taradiddles. He is in fact intangible as the wind. Look for him and you will see nothing; listen, and you will hear nothing. Pray to him, and you will get no answer. The "Tathāgata Śākyamuni" is not a whit more real than any ordinary, workaday apparition'. No wonder that P'eng in his autobiography sadly observes: 'I soon saw that he could not be quickly enlightened.'

Hindu philosophers sometimes divide man's life into four spheres: Dharma (performing the duties of one's caste or profession), Artha (practical business), Kāma (the enjoyments of the senses) and Moksha (striving for spiritual release). Looking at Yuan Mei's life from this point of view it is evident that Dharma, Artha and particularly Kāma all played their part. But Moksha, even using the term in its widest possible sense, does not figure at all.

In the last few years Yuan Mei had been stricken with fever

every autumn, usually in the eighth month. He gives a vivid description of his sensations during one of these attacks: 'When the fever was at its height I had the feeling that there were six or seven people lying scattered about my bed. Sometimes, when I had no inclination to groan, they forced me to do so; or again, when all I wanted to do was to lie still, they would make me toss about. When the fever began to decrease, these intruders became fewer, and when it had completely gone, I went back again to being one single person!'

An incident dating from this year (1755) shows the sort of way in which Yuan Mei risked getting into trouble with the authorities. A member of the Board of Civil Office called Wen was in love with a singing-boy. The boy committed some offence and was put under house-arrest (or strictly speaking, house-boat-arrest) by the Prefect of the southern part of Nanking. This Prefect happened to be Wen's brother and he was much annoyed. Yuan Mei and some friends hired a house-boat that was near to that on which the boy lived, and advanced in solemn procession, as though paying court to a monarch. They drank all night, and one of the friends wrote a number of admiring poems which, before leaving, he slipped into the young singer's sleeve, where they 'lay like silk-worms asleep'.

The early part of 1756 was spent in travelling. He visited Soochow, and went on to Hangchow. Here, coming back from an excursion, he passed the house in Hollyhock Lane where he had lived till he was sixteen. The place by the pond, where he used to sit with his fishing rod, the room that had been his class-room when he was a boy, seemed like things seen in a dream. This year his malaria began somewhat later than usual—in the ninth month—but was very severe. The medicine given by a certain Dr. Lü brought on acute difficulty in breathing. A friend who had sat with him at the special examination in 1736—a certain Chao Ning-ching—called, but was told that Yuan was too ill to see anyone. But Chao explained that he had considerable knowledge of medicine, and was then admitted. He found Yuan on his bed, held up in a sitting posture by his mother, and fighting for every breath. 'He took my pulse, looked at his book of rules and said laughing, "Perfectly easy!" He then sent someone out to buy gypsum and mixed it with some other drug. I had not drunk a spoonful when I felt as though a thousand tons of rock were pressing down upon my intestines. Before I had finished half of the bowl I was sound asleep. . . . When I was dozing off I heard my mother exclaiming, "This must surely be some magic elixir that you have given him". I woke presently to find Chao still sitting beside my bed. "How do you take to the idea of a water-melon?", he asked. "I can't imagine anything I should like better", I said. So someone was sent to buy a water-melon. "I am going now", he said, when the melon arrived. "Just eat as much of it as you fancy." I ate a slice, and it was as though I had been anointed with ambrosia, so airy did my head feel. In the evening I was able to take some gruel. Next day he came again and said, "The malaria you are suffering from is perceptible in the thumb-pulse. Dr. Lü wrongly thought that it was in the wrist-pulse and treated you with astilbe (*sheng-ma*) and angelica (*ch'iang-huo*). That caused a rush of blood upwards. White Tiger Decoction (lime) is the only thing that would cure you; but it too has its dangers."' The thumb-pulse, it should be explained, gives information about the large intestine; one of the wrist pulses gives information about the small intestine.

His concubine Miss T'ao, who had borne him a daughter, died at the age of 29, in 1754. He had in his house a 'waiting-her-time girl' called Phœnix Flute. This name was given to girls who were taken into a household when quite young, with a view to their eventually becoming concubines. But unfortunately Phoenix caught smallpox and when she recovered was much disfigured. Yuan Mei offered her to his brother Yuan Shu and Yuan Shu seems to have been quite willing to take her. But one of his elder sisters dissuaded him, and Yuan Mei handed her on to 'a Mongol general'. He then took as concubine a Miss Lu, who was however by no means the last of his concubines.

To this year belongs a set of 'Chance Stanzas', of which this is one:

If one opens a book, one meets the men of old;
If one goes into the street, one meets the people of today.
The men of old! Their bones are turned to dust;
It can only be with their feelings that one makes friends.
The people of today are of one's own kind,
But to hear their talk is like chewing a candle!
I had far rather live with stocks and stones
Than spend my time with ordinary people.
Fortunately one need not belong to one's own time;
One's real date is the date of the books one reads!

This sounds very 'Ivory Tower' and antiquarian. But, true to the title of this set of poems, he is merely expressing the mood of a particular moment. No one in China took more interest in contemporary literature, particularly poetry, or did more to encourage contemporary writers. Yuan Mei, indeed, knew contemporary poetry much better than he knew the T'ang and Sung poets. He confesses (as we shall see later) that he had never looked at the complete works of Po Chü-i, one of the greatest T'ang poets, till he was seventy. The next poem in the series runs:

I have always been avid of pleasures and entertainments
Of every kind, except games of chance!
I have even endeavoured to enjoy wine and music,
Though in each case without much success.
Every other sort of hobby or enjoyment
I had only to meet with, and at once lost my heart.
But quite suddenly, in my fortieth year,
All other delights began to lose their savour,
And once again, as when I was a child,
I find no pleasure in anything but books.
The moment I wake I long for my library
And bound toward it, swift as a thirsty cat.

I chant aloud the writings of ancient men,
Knowing in my heart that 'moth-eyebrows' is jealous.
What is it that has brought about this change?
I often wonder; but can find no answer.

'Moth-eyebrows', who he knows is 'jealous' because he leaps up and rushes to his books instead of lying late in bed with her, is presumably his new concubine, Miss Lu. The next poem (though the resemblance is no doubt quite fortuitous) has always reminded me of Heine:

I remember of old, when I was a little boy,
Reading my lessons in Hollyhock Lane,
Sometimes our teacher went out to speak to a caller
Letting his pupil scamp the rest of his task.
Then if I heard that the guest had won a degree
I gazed up at him as though he were a king of peaks,
All the family would come to peep and wonder,
Clacking their tongues at this prodigious sight.
Since then twenty years have passed;
What wretched insects they now have all become!
The Bachelors of Arts can hardly paste their mouths;
The Masters of Literature drift from job to job.
At Ching-k'ou the wine is not what it was;
Rice has risen again in Chiang-tung.
And as for high titles and white locks—
One can have one's laugh even at the Duke of Chou.

It was in this year that he addressed a poem to Shen Ch'üan (Nan-p'in), a painter who is fairly well known in China, but who (under the name 'Chin Nanpin') achieved enormous celebrity in Japan. The preface to the poem runs: 'Shen Nan-p'in of Wu-hsing (near Soochow) is well known as a painter. In the Yung Cheng period (1723–1735) the King of Japan brought in his hand a Dwarf (i.e. Japanese) tablet inviting him to his country. He lived there for three years and taught a number of pupils. Then being old and in bad health he came back to China. The King, on his departure, heaped presents upon him. But one of Nan-p'in's fellow travellers had difficulties with the Chinese Customs, and Nan-p'in spent all that he had gained in Japan on helping this man to pay his Customs dues. When he got home, Nan-p'in had not a penny to his name.'

We do not know who invited Shen Ch'üan to come to Japan. We do, however, know that he got on badly with the Japanese at Nagasaki, feeling that they did not make enough fuss about him. At a Mr. Takagi's house he once criticized some pictures by the great Japanese masters Motonobu and Morinobu; but otherwise he mixed very little with the Japanese. So far as we know his only direct pupil was a Nagasaki interpreter called Kumayo Hi. But his paintings were in great demand and exercsied a considerable influence on subsequent 'Chinese Style' painting in Japan. Till his arrival the Japanese knew very little of the contemporary, 'direct from nature' painting in China, and based their style on conventions derived from much earlier Chinese masters. Shen Ch'üan came to Japan at the end of 1731 (i.e. spring 1732, according to the Western calendar) and left in the autumn of 1733. Shortly before he left, the Shogun Yoshimune (Yuan Mei's 'King of Japan') ordered a picture from him. He continued after his return to export pictures to Japan; so he cannot for long have been 'without a penny'. The interest of Yuan Mei's preface is that it illustrates his habitual vagueness about everything connected with foreign peoples and their institutions. Barbarian monarchs of one sort and another did come to the Chinese Court to pay homage; but no Shogun of Japan ever set foot in China, or could conceivably have done so.

A painter friend who was a constant companion of Yuan Mei on his excursions was Li Fang-ying (1695–1754), famous as a painter of plum-blossom. In 1728 his father was presented to the Emperor Yung Cheng. Seeing that he looked old and infirm the Emperor asked if he had any of his sons with him in Peking. 'My fourth son Fang-ying is here', the old man said.

The Emperor asked what post Fang-ying (who was then 37) held at present or would be suitable for. 'He is a licensed student,' said the father, 'but he is not at all clever and I do not think he is up to being an official.' 'One can never tell till one tries', said the Emperor, and Li Fang-ying became Prefect at a succession of places. Everywhere he went he got into trouble for siding with the people against the higher authorities, and at Lan-shan in Hunan he landed in gaol. The local people constantly assembled outside the wall of the prison precincts 'flinging money and provisions to him till the culvert inside the wall was full to the top'. As a painter of plum-blossom he discarded all the inherited 'methods' of brush-stroke, considered essential in depicting plum-blossom, and simply 'painted from nature on his own account'. 'When he went to be temporary Prefect at Ch'u-chou in Anhwei, as soon as he arrived at the place, before seeing any callers, he asked where the plum-tree was that Ou-yang Hsiu (the famous Sung dynasty writer) had planted with his own hand. He was told it was at the Old Drunkard's Arbour. He went there at once, spread a mat and twice prostrated himself before the tree, which happened to be then in blossom.'

'In the nineteenth year of Ch'ien Lung (1754) Li was taken ill and decided to go back to his home in T'ung-chou. After a month or two his servant came with a letter from him in which he said, "Two days after I got home my illness took a bad turn. I am now sending you an account of my career. In life I was unknown; but if someone of your talent were to write something about me when I am dead, it would lighten the darkness of my grave. Could you do it? Written on the second day of the ninth month". I had hardly finished reading the letter when his servant suddenly cast himself weeping at my feet and said, "This was written the day before he died. I held him in my arms while he summoned up his last ounce of strength to write it".'

In the summer of 1758 Yuan Mei's concubine Miss Lu bore him his first son; but the child died. This seems to have given rise to a rumour, current at the time, that Yuan Mei himself had died, and in a poem addressed to Cheng Hsieh (1693–1765) he apologizes for the wasted tears that he had shed on hearing the news of Yuan's death. Cheng (called 'Plank Bridge') was a painter, poet and calligrapher of great originality. He was also famous for his kindness, and it is said that in his latter years he used to carry with him wherever he went a bag full of food and silver bars, so that if he met a friend who seemed to be down-at-heel he might be able immediately to minister to his necessities. The famous modern writer Lin Yu-tang has a particular admiration for Cheng Hsieh and has often spoken of him in his books.

Yuan Mei's daughter A-ch'eng (the child of his first concubine, Miss T'ao) was now fifteen. In the autumn of 1759 a certain Ts'ao Lai-yin made a formal offer for her hand. Yuan was much predisposed in the young man's favour by an antithetical couplet of the would-be son-in-law, quoted to him by the friend who came with the proposal of marriage. It was in praise of Nanking:

Waters up to the Iron Archway stretch their boundless white;
Hills to the very verge of the City carry unbroken green.

Yuan Mei was so pleased with the couplet that he at once consented; but when all the arrangements for the match had been made it was discovered that a Mr. Chiang of Soochow, an old admirer, was still actively courting her, and in the end Yuan Mei (with typical respect for feelings as opposed to formalities) broke off the engagement to the poetical Mr. Ts'ao and married her to Mr. Chiang.

In 1755 the Manchu grandee T'o-yung (born *c.* 1700; died 1773) was given charge of the Imperial Textile Factory at Nanking. He had previously been provincial Treasurer at Canton (1742–1744). Yuan Mei heard that he was deeply versed in Neo-Confucian metaphysics, and imagined him to be a man of narrow and bigoted opinions. But when after five or six years they at last met, they took to each other immediately. 'T'o-yung called next day and as soon as he was seated he asked very gravely whether I would lend him something of mine. "Something very valuable", he said. "I don't know whether you will want to." I could not imagine what he meant. When I asked him, he took out of his sleeve a poem written with the same rhymes as one I had addressed to him the day before. He had incorporated in it unchanged my line "My only regret is that our meeting came six years too late".' For the next four or five years they were close friends, and after T'o-yung left Nanking they continued to exchange affectionate poems till T'o-yung's death in 1773. In the last year of Yuan Mei's life (1797) he wrote:

He had been at Nanking for six years;
But each of us kept aloof from the other.
I was shy of approaching so great a man;
He thought of me as an undisciplined scamp.
To our great surprise when at last we came together
Our only regret was that we had met so late.
He greatly admired my quickness of apprehension
And called me 'The man who guesses with his heart'.
I, for my part, loved his rare refinement;
To be with him was to feel a waft of spring.
When he spoke of the Classics he probed each question to its source;
When he talked about the Way it was always to the point.
The moment his trees were in bloom he bade me come;
And the moon had set before he let me rise. . . .
Then suddenly he went up to Court,
To be President of the Board of Civil Office.
Again and again I got letters from him,
Always saying how it grieved him not to be with me.
And now each time that I go past his garden
I always bow to the tree beneath which he sat.
It only needs a single cry of the crane
To make me think that he is still there.

In about 1765 Yuan Mei wrote an account of four episodes of T'o-yung's earlier life as an administrator. One of these is of particular interest to the Western reader, as it tells the story (seen from the Chinese side) of Commodore Anson's dealings with the Chinese authorities at Canton in 1743. A translation of this account will be found at the end of my book.

The next few years passed very quickly. Yuan Mei felt less and less inclined to leave his books, and in a poem of apology for declining an invitation (1762) he explains to his Manchu patron Yin-chi-shan that 'the mere sound of official drums puts my heart into a panic, and changing into Court shoes brings consternation to my feet'. 'My old eyes', he continues, 'smart when I have to write my name and titles in small script; when called on to write poetry I am afraid of not living up to my reputation.' It will be remembered that Yin-chi-shan had a passion for the literary game of exchanging poems, each writer being compelled to use his antagonist's rhymes. Two years before, the aged ex-official Ch'ien Ch'en-ch'ün (1686–1774) had for a time taken Yuan Mei's place. But in the end, after innumerable rounds of the poetic contest, he wrote to Yin-chi-shan saying: 'I am busy with New Year calls and cannot write any more answering poems. You are at liberty to notify all your friends that old Fragrant Tree (his pen-name) surrendered on the Wukiang road.' Whereupon, to keep Yin-chi-shan in humour, Yuan Mei had once more to step into the breach. To the spring of 1763 belongs the poem:

On a spring night, when I woke from dreams the moon-beams darted chill.
Outside the window, trees in bloom; inside the window, fragrance.
Flowers as though sorry to leave me come to say goodbye;
Half indeed have gone with the wind, but half have climbed into the room.

It is typical of the small, occasional verses that he was writing at this period.

In the autumn of 1764 he had his usual bout of illness, and

there is a curious poem on the theme that 'a man's best friend is his wife'.

I toss about on my hemp-spun sheets, unable to get comfortable;
As age comes, all one's endeavours are spent on nursing one's
health.
It is all very well to buy smiles for a thousand ounces of silver;
One has only to fall ill to find that one's wife is one's truest friend. . .
How touched I am that to get news whether I managed to sleep
You, my lady, do not wait till the cock has crowed twice.

The poems of this period are full of echoes of middle-age. He had taken to dyeing his hair. It had even been suggested to him that he ought to wear spectacles; to which he had replied:

So long as without them I have command of my sight
There is no point in helping it out with 'mirrors'.
Even if they made me see for a thousand leagues
I would rather have nothing between me and my view—
Things that one has to tie to one's nose with a cord
And that form trickles even when one does not weep!
If the Stooping King had not lost a kingdom
Who would have thought worse of him for peering so close?

The 'Stooping King' was the legendary King Yen of Hsu, who lost his kingdom owing to excessive devotion to high moral principles and therefore became a favourite butt of opportunists. According to some accounts he stooped because he had no back-bone; but other accounts (followed here by Yuan Mei) say it was because he was short-sighted. Spectacle lenses in eighteenth-century China were generally made of rock crystal.

His fiftieth birthday (i.e. his forty-ninth in European reckoning) was passed (one cannot say celebrated) on board ship, going from Soochow to Nanking:

The third month came, and I was far from home
When suddenly my fifth decade leapt upon me.

I woke at dawn and remembered it was my birthday—
Sitting alone beside a solitary sail.
My first successes came when I was very young;
I got into the habit of thinking I had plenty of time.
Whenever I met an old person of fifty
I felt 'fifty' to be something that did not concern me,
From which I as yet was infinitely far away,
Separated from it by a thick wad of years.
Yet now suddenly I myself have reached it,
With such terrible speed do years go by.
My early friends, who went into Government posts,
Have all by now done things to be proud of;
There were some who had to wait for their success;
But in middle-age they feel they have met their due.
As for me, what else have I to show
For the years that have passed, save temples streaked with grey?
My Court head-dress has fallen into a parlous state;
All my projects have led to utter rout.
I can look forward to little coming in;
What I saved in the past is now all spent.
Someone found out and started to congratulate me;
I stopped my ears and would not listen to the end . . .
How I envy Feng, Prince of Ying,
The day of whose birth no one could discover!

For the present I am happy to wield a feather fan
While I cross the river, singing the A-t'ung.
To drink my health there are no companions or guests;
To row me on, plenty of hands at the oars.
Wave on wave the grey waters flow;
Gust on gust, the breeze from the distant hills.
There is no one to point at the misty waves and say,
'Out in the offing is an old man of fifty'.

It should be explained that Feng Tao (882–954), a famous opportunist statesman who was posthumously given the title Prince of Ying, having lost his parents when still an infant, was never able to discover the exact date of his birth, and consequently suffered all through life from the handicap of not being able to consult astrologers. The 'boy's song' *A-t'ung* was supposed to date from the third century A.D., and ran:

A-t'ung and again A-t'ung!
Sword in mouth he swam across the river.
He had never feared the tigers on the bank,
But was very frightened of the dragons in the river.

To this time (*c.* 1760–1765) belongs an extremely characteristic letter addressed to Li T'ang, Prefect of the southern part of Nanking: 'Coming back from your office I passed by North Gate Bridge and saw a girl who was handcuffed. She was quite young and very pretty. I asked what she had done, and was told she had been convicted of gambling. The History of the Han Dynasty mentions no less than ten feudal lords who in ancient times gambled away their fiefs, which shows that an addiction to gambling is no new thing. Princes, barons, generals and chief Ministers—all alike have at different times succumbed to it. So what can one expect of a young person brought up in a mean street? The Maker of All Things seems to have no difficulty in producing humans by the million, but the very greatest difficulty in fashioning more than a handful that even have their eyes and noses more or less in the right place. Having found a flower such as this, I should have thought your police would want to protect it from harm, instead of trampling it down like sheep or cattle let loose in a meadow. I asked what she does for a living, and was told she works at a hair-dresser's. I still have a few stray hairs left; so please take her out of her handcuffs at once and have her sent to me, so that I may see whether she is any good at her job. . . .' Yuan Mei, it should be noted, was by no means hostile to Li T'ang, whom he had known since they took their Third Degree together in 1738. 'When we first met', Yuan says, 'we were so different in temperament that we found it hard to get on. But in the end he turned out to be a singularly staunch and faithful friend. When he lay dying, he said, "Yuan Mei is the one person who really understood me. Get him to write my tomb-inscription".' Li T'ang (*c.* 1714–1786) was Prefect of the southern part of Nanking for seven years, and the exact date of the letter is uncertain.

The husband of Yuan Mei's daughter (whose marriage I have mentioned above) died soon after the wedding, and in 1767 Yuan heard that the young widow was gravely ill. He hastened to Soochow where she was living; but before he arrived the news came that she was dead: 'From a thousand leagues away she called to her father; yet he could not see her.' He ends this poem on her death with the reflection that a widow's existence was in any case a wretched one, and perhaps it is all for the best that she died so soon. The girl was, however, only eighteen and second marriages under such circumstances were quite common in China; so it is strange that he should have regarded her as condemned in any case to perpetual widowhood.

In this year his friend Ch'eng Chin-fang (1718–1784) arranged a collection of Yuan's poems. Ch'eng came of a very rich family of salt-brokers. The other members of the family cared only 'for singing-girls, dogs and horses'. Ch'eng Chin-fang had no taste for any of these things and spent his money exclusively on books, collecting a library of fifty thousand volumes and gathering round him scholars from every part of China, with whom he delighted in discussing learned subjects. But towards the middle of the century the fortunes of the Ch'eng family began to decline, and he was obliged to sell most of his books and take a post at Peking. Here he collected another library, fell heavily into debt and died in far-off Shensi, owing Yuan Mei five thousand ounces of silver. This was in 1784. In 1785 his widow buried him at Nanking, and Yuan Mei burnt the bond of debt. 'The sight of a large bench or table', says Yuan, 'was his particular delight, and in a moment he had strewn books and unwound scrolls all over it, forgetting all other business. He delighted too in showering largesse on his friends, sometimes even forcing assistance upon those who had not asked for it. His servants constantly presented him with bills for imaginary expenses, and he allowed them to rob him in this way of almost all he had, without making any attempt to check up on their demands. For all these reasons, although he had his salary and although various friends came to his assistance, it was like trying to block up the ocean with a snow-flake. Mountains of bonds were in the hands of his creditors, and there was no prospect of his being able to meet them. In this plight, he asked for leave, intending to go to Shensi and consult with the Governor of Shensi, Pi Yuan (1730–1797), about how he could make provision for his retirement and old age. At the time he started it was swelteringly hot, he was followed out of the town by duns clamouring for a settlement; old and infirm, he was carried in a covered wheelbarrow, jolting about in the intense heat and getting food and drink only at irregular intervals. To add to all this, news had come that there was a (Moslem) rising on the western frontier and that things looked very bad, which naturally gave him some anxiety. He fell ill, and a month after he reached Pi Yuan's headquarters he died. Alas! The whole Empire teemed with those who were his friends; but it was I who was nearest and dearest to him. Indeed before he went on leave, he wrote to me asking me to find him a house, which delighted me, for I said to myself, "Now I shall not be lonely in my old age".' I have been quoting from the funerary inscription that Yuan Mei wrote for his friend's tomb. He sent this inscription to Pi Yuan, asking him to change it in any way he thought fit. He mentioned, too, that according to the dead man's sister-in-law, Pi Yuan had put aside 3,000 ounces of silver in order to provide for his family in case of Ch'eng's death. 'At present', writes Yuan Mei, 'I am doing what I can for them; but my resources are limited and it is not possible for me to go on helping them indefinitely. . . . I wonder when some fragment of the cloud of your generosity will blow this way?' The means by which Pi Yuan accumulated his fortune were not always very scrupulous; but it cannot be denied that he put it to good use, not only in helping impoverished friends to exist, but also in paying for the printing of their works.

In 1767 the spectacles that he had mocked at two years ago became a necessity. He fished them out of their box, feeling that his being compelled to do so was a melancholy sign of how swiftly old age was stealing upon him. 'For the rest of my life', he says, addressing the spectacles, 'unless it be in your company, I shall not be able to see anything at all.'

His Manchu patron Yin-chi-shan had given up his post of Governor-General at Nanking and gone to Peking to receive a variety of fresh honours. His successor was Kao Chin (1707–1779) whose family was of Chinese origin, but had been given honorary membership of a Manchu clan. In the winter of 1767 Yuan Mei was invited to his house to see theatricals; but what seems to have impressed him most was that in the reception hall there was 'no water-clock or drum', but instead 'a couple of bells that sounded of themselves'. These no doubt were European clocks. European, too, was the contrivance at Yuan Mei's own house, that gave him at this time the greatest pride and pleasure—his mauve glass windows, which to him seemed the last word in up-to-date elegance, though to the Western reader they are more likely to recall the front doors of Victorian suburbia. He had also fixed glass mirrors at an angle outside his windows, so as to have a wider view of what was going on outside, a common practice in Europe at this time. At this party he met his old friend Chiang Ho-ning, with whom he had such exciting discussions about history at Peking in 1739. Chiang, who, it will be remembered (see above, p. 26) was at that time a Courtier in the household of the Emperor's cousin, Prince Ning, was now engaged in writing the official account of the Emperor's Imperial Progresses in the south. During the few months that Chiang Ho-ning was at Nanking, before going south to Changchow to visit his family, the two friends were hardly separated for a moment, so that people said, 'Is there no one you want to see, except Yuan Mei? He clings to you like a mule to its dame'. But they felt that Heaven had given them this one year's intimacy to make up for their thirty years of separation. 'But thirty years is a generation', continues Yuan Mei in his poem of parting. 'One cannot expect to be granted many "generations" in one life-time. . . . I know that you do not drink; but just this once contrive to break your rule. For something must be done to blur the sorrow of such a parting, coupled as it is with the thought that we are both growing old.'

He was plagued at this time, more perhaps than at any period of his life, except during his last illnesses, by the inconveniences of advancing age. A tooth became loose, and he found that its insecurity unbalanced his whole physical economy. He consulted the *Book of Changes*, and obtained omens which he interpreted as meaning 'It will certainly have to be pulled out'. He was introduced to an artificer who promised to make him a false tooth of jade, ground to exactly the right size and attached to the neighbouring teeth by silk threads. It proved to be quite useless for biting on; but

The fellow said, 'It is not meant for that.
You ought to be delighted, not dissatisfied.
The world is full of people with sharp fangs;
But when put to the test, which of them can bite?
This tooth is not intended for chewing food;
It is meant as a screen to protect your mouth from view.
Just try curling your lips in a broad smile;
You will find that no one ventures to say it is false.'

From 1768 too dates a narrative poem addressed to a young actor, Li Kuei-kuan, whom Yuan Mei had met at Soochow the year before. The boy, who was a musician and dancer as well as an impersonator of female roles, devoted every instant of his spare time to reading. He presently obtained a post as dancing-master in the family of a Mr. Chi at Nan-chou in Szechwan; but not wishing to end his days in this obscure and remote post he set out for Peking and was enrolled as one of the official musicians of the Board of Sacrificial Worship. The constraints of this position were already beginning to irk him when at a concert in the town he met Pi Yuan, then an extremely handsome young man of twenty-five. Pi Yuan advanced towards him with a wine-cup, but the boy did not rise. Pi tried to pull him to his feet, asking why he was so unfriendly. 'If you really care for me,' said the boy, 'take me somewhere where we can exchange in private our vows of fidelity. Frankly, I am tired of mountebanking on the stage and making a public exhibition of myself.' They became fast friends; Pi Yuan took the young actor to live with him and they both devoted themselves to study. In 1760 Pi Yuan went in for his Third Degree and was placed first on the list. At the festivities that followed everyone congratulated the boy on Pi Yuan's success in the terms that would have been used in congratulating a successful candidate's wife. Old Shih I-chih (who in 1752 had said to Yuan Mei, 'I hear you have been doing well in your post, but that you do not avoid "the frivolity of Tu Mu"'), gave a party in Pi Yuan's honour and asked after a time if he was not going to be presented to the Top Candidate's 'wife'. Wiping his eyes and viewing the young actor dimly 'like a flower seen through the mist', the aged statesman nodded his approval. Soon afterwards there seems to have been a breach with Pi Yuan (possibly due to Pi's marriage) and the boy went off to the south again, where he lived lavishly and had soon spent all his savings. He came back to Peking, to find that almost all his old associates had vanished. Pi Yuan was still there, but was about to take up a post in Kansu, in the extreme north-west of China. When Yuan Mei met the boy (now about 19) in Soochow in 1767 he was about to throw himself upon the mercy of his former patron, Pi Yuan, by pursuing him to Kansu.

This episode in Pi Yuan's early life has been portrayed in Chapter XII of the early nineteenth-century novel *P'in Hua Pao Chien*, 'Mirror of Stage Beauties'. Chapters LV and LVI describe how a character, who is quite clearly meant as a take-off of Yuan Mei, pretending to take a fatherly and quite detached interest in a young actor's welfare, invites him to come and live with him. The boy sees through his designs and refuses. It is an unpleasant and malicious picture of Yuan Mei in old age, typical of the view that the early nineteenth century in China took of the preceding century and its admired figures. It was unusual at any period for poems such as the one I have summarized above to be printed in a poet's collected works, and in the present case one might have expected that Pi Yuan would be annoyed at its publication. But he does not seem to have minded, and he certainly remained on cordial terms with Yuan Mei till he died in 1797, a few months before Yuan.

In this year (1768) another of Yuan Mei's former associates fell a victim to the savage and arbitrary Literary Inquisition of the Emperor Ch'ien Lung. This was Ch'i Shao-nan, who was one of the fourteen successful candidates at the special examination in 1736, when Yuan Mei failed to pass. He saw something of Ch'i in those early days at Peking, but seldom if ever met him afterwards. After a successful public career Ch'i retired in 1765 to his home at T'ien-t'ai, near the famous monastery-covered hill of that name. But in 1767 a cousin of his called Ch'i Chou-hua was found guilty of having written, forty-three years ago, passages disrespectful to the Manchus and the previous Emperor, Yung Cheng. It transpired that Ch'i Shao-nan had written a preface to one of his cousin's works. Shao-nan was deprived of almost all his possessions, being left only a piece of land worth about five hundred ounces of silver. The affair preyed on his mind, and he fell ill and died in 1768, at the age of sixty-five.

Yuan Mei, though in later years he only occasionally visited Hangchow, never forgot that it was his real home. For a long time past he had been creating a miniature Western Lake in his garden, with some of the features (bridges, peaks, dykes and so on) of the Western Lake near Hangchow. 'If I were still living at Hangchow', he writes, 'I could not spend all day and every day at the Lake. But here I can live at home and yet live beside the Lake; live away from my native place, and yet all the time live there.'

In 1769 his brother Yuan Shu, who held a post in Honan,

had a first son, to whom he gave the child-name A-t'ung. Yuan Mei had several daughters (all born of concubines), but still no son, and his brother suggested to him that he should adopt A-t'ung as his heir, a proposal that he joyfully accepted.

This year Nanking had a new governor called Liu Yung (1719–1804), who was known for the high standards of frugality and propriety that he observed himself and imposed on all members of his family. A rumour got about that Liu Yung had served on Yuan Mei a notice to quit Nanking and return to Hangchow. There were regulations from time to time, designed to check the flow of outside people into the city, and the governor could no doubt have served such a notice. But what really happened is told in the clearest and most convincing way by Yuan Mei himself, both in his *Poetry Talks*, and in several poems written at the time. He says in the *Poetry Talks* that when Liu Yung came to Nanking in 1769 'he had the reputation of being very strict in his views. People looked up to him, but were frightened of him. A rumour got about that he had written to me, ordering me to leave Nanking, and all my neighbours came to say good-bye. My family and his were connected by old ties, but in consequence of these rumours I did not call upon him. Nothing happened till next year, when he sent a Director of Studies, also called Liu, with a letter (couched in very friendly terms) asking me to compose for him a Memorial of thanks to the Emperor for sanctioning the holding of a special examination in Kiangnan in honour of the Dowager Empress's eightieth birthday. It was now obvious that the story that had been going about was entirely without foundation'. But the story that Liu Yung had decided to banish Yuan Mei died hard, and received a further lease of life when, apparently just before Yuan's death, the great scholar Chang Hsueh-ch'eng (1738–1801) gave it further currency in the course of a great diatribe against Yuan, whom he accuses of having perverted the minds of the young by interpreting the Classics in such a way as to make them give support to his own hedonistic views.

At about the same time a school-friend called Shen Jung-ch'ang (to whose daughter Yuan's only son was afterwards married) heard that Yuan had had a stroke, and sent an ointment made with wolf's fat, which was supposed to restore life to paralysed limbs. This rumour too was entirely false; and in this case Yuan seems to have had no idea how it originated.

For seventeen years his father (who died in 1752) had lain in a temporary burial-place. Now a geomancer discovered a 'lucky site' for the final interment barely a hundred steps away from the garden, and the ceremony of reburial took place in the twelfth month of 1769. 'When I was young', Yuan Mei writes, 'my father was away working at secretarial posts in Szechwan and Kwangsi. Afterwards I was taking examinations at Peking, and we were constantly separated. Now this garden has brought us together again. Here he will lie, here receive his offerings, here have his tomb. Father and son will never again be apart for a single day.' This last sentiment must not be taken too literally; for it was his habit to spend part of almost every year away from Nanking, at Yangchow or Soochow, and later on he travelled more and more. From this year dates a poem called *The Bell*:

No monk lives at the old temple, the Buddha has toppled to the floor;
One bell hangs high, bright with evening sun.
Sad that when only a tap is needed, no one now dares
To rouse the notes of solemn music that cram its ancient frame.

In 1771 his Manchu patron and friend Yin-chi-shan died at the age of seventy-five, and was buried far away in Manchuria, in the burial-ground of his clan. Manchus who went in for a military career lived and died as Manchus. But a cultivated Manchu like Yin-chi-shan, who was a member of the Han-lin Academy and had taken his Third Degree in 1723, who had a passion for Chinese literature and Chinese literary pastimes, seems when we read Yuan Mei's numerous anecdotes about him to be a typical eighteenth-century Chinese gentleman;

and it is strange to think of him being laid to rest with pagan rites, far beyond the Great Wall. When after being Governor-General on and off for thirty years he left Nanking in 1765, Yuan Mei travelled north with him as far as the junction of the Grand Canal with the Yellow River. Their parting was to be early in the morning. Yuan got up in good time and was washing his face, when a messenger arrived saying that Yin-chi-shan had already started. He could not face the final farewell.

This year, visiting Hangchow, Yuan called a sedan-chair and noticed that the carrier was looking at him curiously. 'I can't help thinking we have met before', the man said:

The chair-carrier wiped his eyes and looked,
And looked again, and heaved a deep sigh.
He told me that on the day of my wedding
He was one of those that carried the Bridegroom's Chair.
'Brisk you were, a little Han-lin scholar,
Your young cheeks rosy as the morning glow.
Why have we not seen you for so long
That then you were a boy and now are an old man? . . .'
He broke off; but before he had finished speaking
A great depression suddenly came upon me.
It was like meeting an aged T'ien-pao man
Telling again the yellow-millet dream.

The allusions in the last two lines, though a Western reader obviously needs an explanation, are not (as they might appear to be) learned or obscure. The T'ien-pao period (A.D. 742–755) came just before one of the great 'divides' in Chinese history—the revolution of An Lu-shan, which almost overthrew the T'ang dynasty. To the survivors of the revolution the T'ien-pao era, with all its gaieties and splendours, seemed as unreal as a dream. Even at the beginning of the ninth century one sometimes met 'an old man of T'ien-pao still telling the glories of a vanished reign'. With this allusion Yuan Mei has combined one to what is often called 'the dream at Han-tan'.

A young man going up to the Capital to try his fortune orders supper at an inn. While he is waiting for the millet to be cooked he falls asleep, his head propped on a pillow given to him by another guest. He dreams that he comes to the Capital, takes his Degree, is promoted from one high post to another, gets into trouble and is degraded, is recalled to office, endures the hardship of distant campaigns, is accused of treason, condemned to death, saved at the last moment, and finally dies at a great old age. Awakening from his dream he discovers that the millet is not yet cooked. In a moment's sleep he has lived through the vicissitudes of a great public career. Convinced that in the world 'honours are followed by disgrace and praise by calumny' he turns back towards the village from which he came. The pillow was a magic pillow, and the other guest a Taoist magician.

I have in general not translated poems containing allusions of this kind, for by the time the reader has coped with the necessary explanations he is likely to have lost the mood in which one reads a poem as a poem, rather than as a document. But allusion is so common in Yuan Mei's, as in most other Chinese poetry, that I wanted to give at least one example showing how he handles it.

In 1772 he arranged more than 1,900 poems and other compositions sent to him by friends and acquaintances all over China during the last forty years. He was also busy writing poems for other people. His doctor Hsiang-shan Tzu asked for a poem to celebrate his fortieth birthday, with the special proviso that no mention was to be made of the fact that he was a doctor, because 'ordinary people look down on doctors'. They were indeed despised partly because they were specialists, and the Confucian gentleman was supposed only to have a knowledge of generalities; partly, as we have seen, because they were regarded as sharing the discredit that attached to *shamans* and wonder-workers of all kinds. Yuan Mei begins his poem by protesting that the Confucian Way and the principles governing crafts like medicine were one and the same. He then strings together a long series of legendary and poetic allusions to 'healing', in the course of which the forbidden word 'doctor' occurs over a dozen times.

The summer was so hot that few people had the energy to call:

My hill is deserted; in this hot weather I live behind closed doors,
I am dressed only in the thinnest gauze, but still my sweat streams.
There is one good thing: this hot wind prevents people from calling;
In the long day I have time to add line after line to my book.

If he is here referring to any particular book it would perhaps be his Jottings (*Sui Pi*), which I shall discuss later.

A young actor called Li, who had served in Yin-chi-shan's household, called one day and Yuan took him to the room where he kept old letters, and they went through the notes that Yin-chi-shan had sent to Yuan. Most of these had been brought round by Li, who was deeply devoted to Yin-chi-shan:

I saw that your eyes were red with weeping the moment you entered the gate.
I know well how sad you feel when you think of those old days.
Coming back after ten years to the house you know so well
You wonder whether you are in my garden or only in a dream.

In 1772 or 1773, in order to 'avoid somebody', i.e. get out of his jurisdiction, Yuan Mei set out for a farm on the other side of the Yangtze, that he had purchased some fifteen years ago. It would appear that the new Governor of Nanking, Chung Kuang-yu, who succeeded Liu Yung in 1770, had actually done what his predecessor was falsely supposed to be going to do, that is to say, had issued an expulsion order against Yuan Mei. Nothing seems to be known about the new Governor, nor does Yuan Mei give any further information about the episode, except that after setting out across the Yangtze, he almost immediately turned back. In a poem written on leaving he consoles himself with the thought that 'poets have always been fond of house-moving'. What happened to enable him to go back almost as soon as he started, we do not know. It is possible that the new Governor had in his turn been succeeded by Ch'ien Chin-tien, who was Governor till 1775.

Yuan's concubine Miss Chin's younger sister Feng-ling had been sold as a slave to a rich family. Yuan Mei ransomed her and brought her to live under her sister's care. The child (for when she came she was only 13) was very pretty, and Yuan became deeply attached to her. But it seemed to him that he ought to provide for her future, and much against his inclination he found her a husband at Soochow. At the farewell meal when she was about to be carried away, Yuan sat with his back to her lest she should see that he was weeping and herself 'mount the bridal carriage with tears in her eyes', which would of course have been an evil omen. But she had only gone to him as a secondary wife, and the husband's 'great wife' treated her so harshly, taking away her rings and combs and keeping her on short rations, that she soon 'drooped like an ailing butterfly', and in the end hanged herself in despair. Yuan naturally reproached himself bitterly for having sent her away.

In the summer of 1773 he saw at Yangchow the first performance of *Four Strings at Autumn*, the play by his friend Chiang Shih-ch'üan that I have mentioned above (p. 73). As this was the *première* of the most famous Chinese drama of the eighteenth century it would have been interesting if Yuan Mei had given some account of the impression made upon him by the *Four Strings* as a play. But he was more interested in the young actor Hui Lang who played the part of the Lute Girl, than in the play itself. The story of the play, briefly, is that when the poet Po Chü-i was in exile at Kiukiang on the Yangtze, while he was seeing off a visitor who was leaving by boat, he heard someone in the cabin of a neighbouring boat singing not in the local, southern style, but in the style of the north-west, where the Capital was. He went alongside and asked the singer to come on to his boat. He then learnt that she was a famous singer of the Capital, who had fallen on evil days and had ended by marrying a tea-merchant. The merchant was frequently away on business and she led an unhappy life, brooding on her former triumphs. Po Chü-i, who has never up till now felt lonely in his exile, is deeply moved by her recollections of the Capital, and bursts into tears.

On the stage, the Lute-girl sings from behind a screen, to indicate that she is inside her boat-cabin. Hui Lang, playing the role of the girl, is seen at first only as a slender shadow behind the screen. Then he is heard warbling the song:

The wind blowing the willow-catkins fills the inn with scent;
Girls from Wu bring cup on cup, clamouring that I must drink.
I wonder if the waters of the river flowing to the east
Know as they hurry away and away such bitter pangs as mine.

Yuan Mei writes of this moment of the play:

Hui Lang slim and graceful, a solitary shadow,
Pours from his throat that shrill song behind the painted screen,
Much like the mango-bird that veers to the highest tree,
Not wanting to be approached, but wanting to be heard.

In 1773 he heard that his friend Ch'eng Chin-fang (the rich salt-merchant's son who managed his own financial affairs so badly) had been made an assistant editor of the texts which were to be collected to form the Complete Library (*Ssu-ku Ch'üan-shu*) which was the greatest literary enterprise of Ch'ien Lung's reign. There is no reason to doubt that it was in the main a learned undertaking. But it soon became one of the chief instruments of the Literary Inquisition. Of the books sent in for inclusion in the library thousands were burnt because they were judged to contain passages hostile to the Manchu dynasty, and there were many prosecutions. Yuan

Mei was probably rather hurt that he too had not been asked to assist in this enterprise:

I still do not seem to avoid being classed as an ignoramus,
Narrow in what I have heard and seen, careless in my researches.
I turn and look towards the City and in vain heave my sigh;
If only I might come and join you, and drudge as your secretary!
As it is, what you might *do is to send me a list of the titles,*
Then I should have some vague idea of what is going on,
And should not feel that I gain nothing by living under a sage's rule.

At this period (*c.* 1773) he was beginning to receive very large sums for his writings. Speaking in his Will (1797) of sums paid to him for literary compositions, Yuan says, 'I sometimes got as much as a thousand ounces of silver (about £300 in eighteenth-century English money) for one tomb-inscription. But literary patrons such as Tung Shih-min and Pao Chih-tao were of course rare'. The first of the two inscriptions referred to here is printed in Volume 31 of his Prose Works. It is an inscription for the tomb of Tung Shih-min's mother, who died in 1773. It is a document of only about 800 words, so that the rate of remuneration is, even according to modern American standards, fantastically high. Pao Chih-tao (1743–1801) was a much later patron. In his case the document referred to is an account of Pao Chih-tao's father, written in 1795. The implication would appear to be that he got a thousand ounces of silver for this work also. It is a mere four pages. Pao Chih-tao started as a clerk in a tea-store. By immense industry and application he saved up enough to set up on his own as a salt merchant. He became the most famous philanthropist of his day, endowing numerous public works, academies and so on.

If a thousand was the maximum, one may reasonably suppose that he often got from 300 to 500 ounces for literary works. He also earned a lot from his books. He paid wood-engravers about 3s. 4d. per double page. In this initial expense he was sometimes helped by friends. The blocks became his property and were kept in an upper room, where copies were printed off as required, the printers coming to his house to do the work. He was thus his own publisher. But there was nothing to prevent book-sellers from re-engraving them, if they thought it worth their while. From these commercial copies, generally poorly printed on cheap paper, he got no profit at all, though they gave him the satisfying assurance that his works were in general demand.

His own library did not, of course, escape the attention of the 'book officials', and he agreed to present all the rarer books and MSS he possessed to the new Imperial Library. He also took this opportunity of getting rid of all the works that were of purely philological interest. In future he was determined to read only to 'get the general sense', without going into textual details. 'In this dynasty', he says, 'far too many people have devoted their talents to text-collation.'

In the spring of 1774 he went for an excursion towards Hangchow with a young actor Kuei Lang. After five days his companion left him to fulfil an engagement at Nanking and Yuan, at his inn, felt very desolate, and could not sleep:

In the casual life of meetings and partings there is much sadness to endure;
A five-days' entanglement, and then what comes?
The moonlit gardens of Nanking tonight are white as snow;
Would that I could hear but one note of the songs the fair one is singing!

However, in the next poem in the series, another actor, Ts'ao Lang, has taken Kuei Lang's place, and is accompanying him to Chinkiang.

In 1774 an old acquaintance called T'ao I came as Governor to Nanking. He was there for less than a year, but he and Yuan became great friends and continued to correspond after T'ao I went on to a post at Canton. On the new Governor's desk he found copies of some of his own early poems which he had suppressed. He took them away, gave them a 'brush up' and brought them back to T'ao I, explaining that 'a flower plucked too early in the day cannot have its full fragrance'.

On New Year's Eve, 1774, he wrote the following poem:

On this night year after year I have listened eagerly,
Never missing a single sound of the crackers till dawn came.
But this year on New Year's Eve I cannot bring myself to listen,
Knowing that when the cock crows I shall enter my sixtieth year.
The mighty din of the celebrations has already died away;
If a little time is still left, it is only a last scrap.
But the cock, as though feeling for my plight, is slow to open its mouth,
And I that write this am still a man of fifty-nine!

When the dramatist Chiang Shih-ch'üan settled in 1765 at Nanking, in a house close to Yuan Mei's, he brought with him his mother, who became great friends with Yuan Mei's mother. 'The two old people,' Yuan says (though Chiang's mother was then only fifty-nine), 'finding themselves such close neighbours and having similar tastes, enjoyed going about together. But after a short time Chiang Shih-ch'üan was called to the Chi-shan Academy at Shao-hsing, and took his mother with him. My mother missed her terribly and used to say that being parted from Mrs. Chiang was like losing the spring wind. In the first month of this year (1775) Mrs. Chiang died at Yangchow, and Chiang Shih-ch'üan wrote to me at once asking me to compose her tomb-inscription. I knew that the news would upset my mother, and it was some time before I dared to break it to her. Considering the place that Chiang himself holds in literature and that he is on familiar terms with all the great writers of the day, I wondered at first why he had sent from a distance to me of all people to write this inscription. In the end I came to the conclusion that his mother's great love for my mother had perhaps given her a particular feeling for me, and that before she died she had expressed a wish that I should write about her.'

This year (1775) Yuan Mei, who still had no son, adopted A-t'ung, the child of his brother Yuan Shu. When deposited 'on a pile of ten thousand books' the child chortled with delight, which was taken as an omen that he would inherit his new father's tastes. But visitors persisted in thinking that so young a child must surely be a grandson.

In this year he completed a collection of his works, both prose and verse, and had it printed, that 'for a thousand autumns, ten thousand eyes may read it'. I do not know if any copies of this edition still exist.

Yuan Mei took being sixty very seriously, and even made up his mind that he was too old to write poetry. 'I meant', he wrote years afterwards to Ch'ing-lan, the son of Governor-General Yin-chi-shan, 'to give up writing poetry when I was sixty.' He decided, however, that poetry is an expression of feeling and even at sixty one has feelings that are entirely of one's own. Where old men are apt to fail is in writing about their concrete surroundings, which are the same for everybody:

The oriole, when old, ought not to trill its tongue;
Men, when old, ought not to write poetry.
In most cases their vigour has departed
And even at the best they can only repeat themselves.
Po Chü-i and Lu Yu as well
Might have done better to stop before they did.
And how much more is it true of such as I!
One must be on one's guard against going on and on.
All the same, things happen that move me,
And unbidden my lips begin to stir.
Every year fresh poems come
Just as the flowers come back at every spring.
I have an idea that an old man's poems
Should talk of feelings and not talk of scenes.
Scenes are what all people share;
Feelings are a single person's property.

A very curious poem, having some affinity with the preceding one, is entitled 'Inscription for a painting of the Yellow Millet Dream-pillow'; that is to say, the dream at Han-tan, the theme that he used in the poem about his dream-like return to Hangchow (see above, p. 103):

Without Concept, without Cause, dreams are hard to understand;
Each man's inward passions are his and his alone.
I once passed through Han-tan and had a dream there;
I dreamt I opened a scroll of writing amid ten thousand flowers.

The terms in the first line are Buddhist. 'Concept' is the Sanskrit *samjñā* and 'Cause' is *hetu*. Yuan seldom uses Buddhist terms; but it seems evident that he here intends the words in a Buddhist sense. The 'flowers' are certainly 'amours', as so often in his poems. But the quatrain is 'hard to understand', and would indeed defeat its purpose if it were not.

Towards the end of 1777 he completed the first instalment (in fifteen chapters) of his 'Jottings' (*Sui Pi*). He went on adding to the book until the end of his life. When it was printed, some years after his death, it had grown to nearly twice the original size. Most scholars, both in China and in the West, make notes on the books they read, and the problem arises, what to do with them? As Yuan Mei himself says, when they have reached a certain bulk, 'one is reluctant to keep them and equally reluctant to throw them away'. In the West, some of them get incorporated in books or learned articles, and others come in handy when reviewing books in specialist periodicals. I once asked the great French scholar Paul Pelliot why he wasted his time reviewing so many obviously worthless books. He said it was the only available way of utilizing the voluminous *fiches* that he had accumulated in the course of years. The Chinese had no learned periodicals in the eighteenth century. To some extent their place was taken by letters exchanged between learned friends and often copied and passed round. Yuan Mei carried on a vast correspondence of this kind, and we often find him utilizing in it the notes in his *Sui Pi*. But it had long been a common practice in China to print jottings of this kind, either pell-mell just as they stood, or else (as in the case of Yuan Mei's book) arranged under a series of headings. For purposes of serious study such books (unless indexed) are almost useless; and it was not till recent times that any of them were indexed. Another disadvantage of such works was that they inevitably consisted to a large extent of small discoveries that (unknown to their author) had constantly been made before. Western scholarship now demands that before writing on a subject an author must know everything that has been written on it in every part of the globe. This demand is theoretically unassailable; but it has the practical disadvantage of involving the scholar, before he can set pen to paper, in preliminary researches that may last for years, at the end of which he may merely reach the conclusion that nothing has been written on his subject that has any contemporary value at all.

It would only be possible to deal with individual points in Yuan Mei's *Sui Pi* if one were writing for readers who know Chinese, and if one could use Chinese characters. Here I can only give some general indications of Yuan's methods as a scholar. He lived in an age when belief was crumbling. The Confucian Classics, instead of being regarded as sacred writings beyond the reach of textual criticism, were beginning to be examined and discussed as though they were ordinary ancient texts. The result was that many of them, formerly attributed to Confucius or to his disciples, were found to be of much later date and consequently of much less authority. In this process the most sensational event was the final and unanswerable demonstration by Yen Jo-chü (1636–1704) in a book that was first printed and became generally known in 1745, that a considerable part of the venerated *Book of History*, supposed to date from many hundred years B.C., was in fact a forgery of the fourth century A.D. Yuan Mei was aware of these new developments, in so far as they had become generally accessible, and his approach to the Classics was that of the more advanced scholars of his day. But he never examined any learned question systematically or exhaustively, and many of his comments, though made in the rationalistic spirit of the day and perhaps nearer truth than the traditional views, are obviously superficial and incomplete. In connection with Yuan's notes and other writings on the Classics, a word may be said here about his general philosophy of life. The two subjects are closely akin, because every Chinese writer who put forward views of his own felt bound to justify them by quotations from the Classics. If he could find no passage that supported his view, then he was obliged to wrest some phrase from its context and misinterpret it in a way that justified his contentions. The basic idea on which Yuan Mei's whole philosophy rests is that whatever can be sensuously enjoyed is given to us by Heaven for our delight, and that we are impiously flouting Heaven if we refuse to take advantage of it to the full, or prevent others from doing so. How other people fulfil their duty to Heaven in this respect is indeed no one's business but their own. There must be no 'hiding under beds and spying into private affairs'. I have spoken of Yuan's 'philosophy', but this is perhaps too grand a term. One would expect a philosopher to deal with the main difficulties that adoption of his system would entail. To explain, for example, in Yuan's case, what is to happen if my exploitation of Heaven's gifts interferes with someone else's. But so far as I know, he never does this, and perhaps it would be better merely to speak of his 'outlook'.

A passage in *The Great Learning* (one of the 'Four Books') says that the sage ruler does not let a plaintiff who is 'without facts' to support his case go on indefinitely with his plea. The word *ch'ing*, 'facts', has in other contexts the meaning 'feelings', 'passions', and Yuan Mei in one of his essays perverts the sentence into meaning 'a man without sensual passions cannot express himself to the full', and quotes it as a justification for his hedonistic view of life. It was, I think, sophistries of this kind, rather than his actual mode of life, that caused him to be regarded as a danger to his pupils. They certainly dispose of any idea that he is to be taken very seriously as a philologian.

The cultivated and sympathetic T'ao I, who had for all too short a time been Governor of Nanking, went on being raised from one important post to another. He and Yuan Mei continued to correspond, and in 1777 T'ao sent him a present most suitable to an elderly beau—a bottle of very special hair-dye. In his letter of thanks Yuan Mei mentions the fact that the Emperor had been showering honours upon T'ao I. But a year later T'ao I died in gaol, another victim of the Literary Inquisition. In the summer of 1778 the Bureau of Censorship at Nanking was called upon to deal with the writings of a certain Hsu Shu-k'uei. The censors were at the time so overwhelmed with suspect literature that they put the case aside. In the autumn Liu Yung, who when Governor of Nanking was falsely supposed to have been going to banish Yuan Mei, acting in his capacity of Commissioner for Education in Kiangsu, called the attention of the Emperor to the fact that this case had not been dealt with as promptly as it should have been. Certain verses in a poem by Hsu Shu-k'uei were regarded as a covert attack upon the Manchu dynasty. Whether they were actually intended in this sense is now impossible to judge, as the poem in which they occur no longer survives, and to make a final judgment one would have to read them in their context. But it is certain that the couplet which is quoted can only be interpreted as seditious by doing violence to ordinary Chinese idiom. A special enquiry found that the case had been dealt with negligently by the officials concerned, one of whom was Yuan Mei's friend T'ao I. He was sentenced to imprisonment, and, as I have said, died in gaol. Hsu Shu-k'uei himself was executed and his corpse dismembered. That T'ao I, who was now an elderly man, should not have survived imprisonment is not surprising. Fang Pao (1668–1749), who in 1711 was accused of having written a preface to a book containing seditious matter has, in his *Yü-chung Tsa Chi* ('Notes on Prison Life') left a terrifying picture of a Peking gaol. Over two hundred prisoners were housed in dungeons that had no apertures either for light or ventilation. At nightfall the prisoners were locked in 'along with their excrements', so that the stench became appalling. Sometimes as many as ten prisoners a day died and were pushed out through a kind of oubliette.

After T'ao I's death (how long afterwards we do not know) Yuan Mei wrote an account of a number of cases tried by him early in his official career, in which he showed singular fairness and sagacity. By doing so Yuan probably ran a considerable risk of being prosecuted himself.

At last, in the autumn of 1778, Yuan had a son, born to him by his concubine Miss Chung. He called him A-ch'ih, which means 'the late one'. But as we have seen he had already made his nephew A-t'ung his heir, and this arrangement remained unaltered. Next year, accompanied by Miss Chung and another concubine, he took the child to Hangchow, to present it to the spirits of its ancestors at the family burial-place. He had still many relatives at Hangchow and describes himself as being surrounded by aunts and sisters, all of them now 'semi-crones, with flowing white locks'. He promised them all that he would bring his little boy A-ch'ih to see 'the Emperor in his coach and the glitter of fireworks in the sky'; for another Imperial tour in the South was planned for 1784. He returned to Nanking with a 'a cartload of ghosts'; that is to say new ghost-stories for use in the collection that he had for some time past been composing.

At the beginning of 1780 there was a heavy fall of snow, Yuan Mei and his family set to work to store snow in a shed, for use in the summer:

All my life moonlight and snow are the things I have loved best;
Nothing can be done to keep the moon, one can only let it wane.
But the snow, more friendly than the moon, has come to be my guest.
All things that Heaven bestows we ought gratefully to receive.
On the first night of this year the snow never stopped.
At break of day I rolled up my sleeves and went straight to work.

I made the gardener call the maids and bring my old wife.
We washed out tubs, set jars in a row and a great assortment of buckets. . . .

It will last, Yuan Mei says, far into the summer and be far handier than the ice-blocks for which rich people pay so heavily. There will be enough of it 'to comfort every fevered brow in the world'.

He had again been having malaria, and for the time being was feeling very elderly and decrepit:

On my walks I continually pause, and at home am absent-minded;
I have the feeling that this time old age has come for good.
I can't remember where I have put things and have to write it down;
I still delight in looking at hills, but leave it to others to climb them.
My sleep is short, never lasting beyond the third watch;
My appetite has gone, I cannot manage more than a handful of rice.
All in all, what is it like to be an ageing man?
A last patch of spring snow, a candle when dawn has come.

And again:

Half an hour of conversation, and I feel quite upset;
Before I have walked three steps I think of hailing a chair.
All that is left me is a pair of roving eyes, in avid search
For the stray flowers that here and there lurk amid the world's mist.

Here as usual, of course, the flowers are people.

A compensation for old age was that the style of hat and robe that he had adopted thirty years ago and stuck to obstinately ever since had now, by a turn of the wheel of fashion, become modish again:

The length of coats and the width of hats in the last thirty years
Time and again have chopped and changed in a quite senseless way.
Happily for me I have always stuck to the same old style
And, looking about me, I find I am dressed in the very latest fashion.

In the spring of 1778 his mother died at the age of ninety-three. She was quiet, undemonstrative, sceptical. 'She did not keep fasts or pay court to Buddha. She did not believe in *yin-yang* magic, nor in prayer. When not busy with needle-work, she liked to take a volume of T'ang poems and chant them to herself. . . . When she felt that she was dying, she sent for me to say goodbye. "I am going to leave you", she said. Involuntarily I let a cry of dismay escape my lips. "Don't be silly", she said. "Surely you have had enough of me by now! Everyone has to die sometime, and I am ninety-three. You must not be sad about it." She raised her sleeve to wipe away my tears, and fell back dead.' 'Long after my own hair was grey she went on treating me as though I were a child. When I went to her room she never failed to give me a sweetmeat or a slice of melon, make sure if it was hot that I was not too warmly dressed, or if it was cold, that I was well wrapped up, and to satisfy herself that I was getting wholesome things to eat and drink. I, of course, played up to her view of me as a small child, and ended by quite forgetting that I was a battered old man. Indeed it was not till I lost her that I fully realized I was a man of sixty-two.'

In this year there were bad floods on the Yellow River. Whenever a breach in the banks had been repaired and the officials were congratulating themselves that all would now be well, a flock of green wild-geese suddenly appeared, skimming over the face of the water, and that night the new embankment would give way. When shot at with fowling-pieces they would scatter, but soon come back in force. 'Not even the oldest river-conservancy workers', says Yuan Mei, 'knew what the birds really were. But in the *Kuei-hai Pai-pien* I found the statement that during the rebellion of Huang Hsiao-yang (A.D. 1449) the Yellow River was haunted by green birds which were identified as Fou-ni ("floating nuns"), which is the name of a kind of water-goblin. Someone said that the thing to do was to sacrifice a black dog to them and throw to them ribbons woven with threads of five different colours. This was tried, says the *Kuei-hai Pai-pien*, and the creatures disappeared.'

In 1781 his daughter Feng-ku married a grandson of Shih I-chih, who supervised the teaching of the Han-lin scholars in 1740, and had at that time and afterwards showed great kindness to Yuan Mei. The Shih family lived at Li-yang, not far from Li-shui where Yuan Mei had held his first post. Feng-ku, Yuan himself tells us, was no great beauty, but she was clever, and he had been using her as his 'lady-secretary':

Whenever I was baffled by an unusual character
It was her job to look it up in the dictionary.
Whenever I wanted to hear a strange story
It was she who found it in the wonder-books.

Yuan Mei had a friend called Lo P'ing (1731–1819), who was famous for his paintings of ghosts and apparitions. But he also painted a portrait of Yuan Mei: 'Lo P'ing painted a portrait of me. But my family denies that it is me, and these two views seem impossible to reconcile. . . . It is hard to take a true view of oneself, but equally hard to take a true view of one's own productions. I may not know what I look like; but does Lo P'ing know any better what his picture looks like? . . . As my family says it is not me, if we keep it here it may be wrongly identified. Someone may well think it is a sketch of the old man who helps in the kitchen or of the pedlar who comes round with lemonade, and may take it upon himself to tear it up or throw it away. . . . That is why I am not venturing to keep it, but am sending it back to Lo P'ing to look after for me, so that everyone who knows me and who knows

Lo P'ing may be able to have a good look at it.' On one of Lo P'ing's ghost (demon) pictures he wrote the inscription:

I am compiling a book of ghosts and wonders,
Giving it the title 'What the Master did not speak of'.
And now seeing this ghost picture of yours
I have learnt a lot that I did not know before.
I fancy today no one else exists
So well up in the subject as you and I.

A first draft of Yuan's vast collection of 'strange stories' was probably finished by the end of this year (1781). A sequel was published about 1796. Its title, 'What the Master did not talk of' (*Tzu pu yü*) refers to the passage in the seventh book of the *Analects* of Confucius: 'The Master never talked of wonders, feats of strength, disorders of nature or spirits.' The book contains many ghost-stories in our sense of the term, but also accounts of unusual experiences of every description. It is headed 'written in the Sui Yuan for entertainment.' The Chinese had an insatiable appetite for wonder-tales, and collections of them had been made since very early times. Sometimes they had, as in Russia, been made the vehicle for attacks upon the government of the day, or for moral instruction or for putting forward unorthodox views. But with one or two exceptions Yuan Mei's wonder-tales seem to be accounts of actual psychic experiences, as communicated to him by friends and contemporaries, and in some cases as experienced by himself or his family. There is no attempt to give them coherence or literary structure, and for that reason they shed an interesting light on the psychic background of cultivated people at the time. Viewed, however, simply as literature they are likely to strike a Western reader as too irrational and inconsequent. Here is one such tale:

A certain Mr. Yeh had a friend called Wang, and on Wang's sixtieth birthday Yeh mounted his donkey and rode off to congratulate Wang. At dusk, when he was crossing the Fang Shan (south-west of Peking), he was caught up by a big fellow on horseback, who asked him where he was going. When Yeh told him, he said, 'How fortunate! Wang is my cousin and I too am going to visit him on his birthday. Let us keep each other company!' Yeh was delighted to have a companion, and readily assented. After a time he noticed that the big fellow continually lagged behind. He invited him to lead the way, and the other pretended to accept the suggestion. But in a few minutes he had fallen behind again. Yeh began to suspect that the man was a bandit and kept on glancing at him over his shoulder. It was soon pitch dark, and he could no longer see his companion. But presently a storm began, there was a flash of lightning and by its light Yeh saw that the fellow was now hanging from his saddle head downwards, his feet moving in space, as though he were walking; and at every step he took there was a peal of thunder, each thunder-clap being also accompanied by a black vapour which issued from the fellow's mouth. Yeh saw that he had an immensely long tongue, red as cinnabar. He was of course much startled and alarmed; but there seemed to be nothing for it but to ride on as fast as he could to Mr. Wang's house. Wang was delighted to see them both and at once asked them to have a drink. Taking Wang aside, Yeh asked him if it was a fact that he was related to the person he had met on the road. 'Oh yes', said Mr. Wang. 'That's quite right. It's my cousin Mr. Chang. He lives in Rope-makers Lane at Peking and is a silversmith by profession.' This reassured Yeh, and he began to think that what he had seen during the night was simply an hallucination. However, when the time came for going to bed, he did not much like the idea of sharing a room with the fellow. But the other insisted upon it and Yeh was obliged reluctantly to concur, only taking the precaution of getting an old servant of Mr. Wang's to sleep in the same room. Yeh could not manage to get to sleep. At the third watch, though the candle had gone out, the whole room was suddenly filled with light, and Yeh saw the man sitting up in bed; the light came from his huge protruding tongue. He then came over and sniffed at Yeh's bed-curtains, saliva dripping from his jaws. But seeming to realize that Yeh was awake, he changed his mind and seizing the old servant, devoured him almost to the last bone. It so happened that Yeh was a devotee of Kuan Yü, the God of War, and he now hastened to call out: 'Great Sovereign, subduer of demons, where are you?' At once there was a resounding boom as though a gong had been struck, and Kuan Yü appeared from between the rafters, with a huge sword in his hand. He struck at the monster, who at once turned into a butterfly as big as a cart wheel and spread its wings to parry the blow. After the combatants had pranced round one another for a moment or two, there was a loud crash, and both the butterfly and the god vanished.

Yeh fell fainting to the floor and was still lying there when at noon Mr. Wang came to see what had happened to him. He had now recovered sufficiently to tell Wang the whole story, and Wang indeed saw for himself that there was fresh blood on the servant's bed. But both Mr. Chang and the servant had disappeared, though Chang's horse was still in the stable. They at once sent a messenger to Peking, who on reaching Chang's workshop found him at his stove melting silver. He had been in Peking all the time and had never gone to Mr. Wang's to congratulate him on his sixtieth birthday.

Here is another story:

In the year *Hsin-mao* of the Ch'ien Lung period (1771) my brother Yuan Shu went to the Capital in company with his examination-mate Shao. They reached Luan-ch'eng on the 21st of the fourth month. All the inns at the Eastern Barrier were crammed with travellers and their equipages. But presently they found an inn where there seemed to be no guests at all, and decided to stay here for the night.

Shao took the outer room and my brother the inner room. When it was beginning to get late they went to bed each in his own room, but kept the lamps burning and continued for a time to talk to each other through the partition wall. Suddenly my brother saw a man about ten feet high, with a green face and green whiskers, dressed and shod all in green, come in at the door. He was so tall that his hat made a rustling sound as it brushed against the paper of the top-light in the ceiling. Soon a dwarf not so much as three feet high also appeared at my brother's bedside. He had a very large head, and he too had a green face, and was dressed all in green. He moved his sleeves up and down, and postured like a dancer. My brother tried to call out, but found he could not open his mouth. Shao was still talking to him from the next room but he was unable to say anything in reply. To add to his bewilderment another man now appeared, sitting on the low stool beside his bed. He had a pock-marked face and a long beard; on his head was a gauze cap, and he was wearing a very wide belt. He pointed at the giant and said to my brother, 'He's not a ghost'. Then he pointed to the dwarf with a big head, and said, 'But that one is'. Then he waved his hand towards the giant and the dwarf, saying something that my brother could not catch. They both nodded and began to salute my brother with their hands folded in their sleeves. At each salute they retreated one step. The last salute brought them to the door, and they disappeared through it. The man with the gauze cap then saluted in the same way, and also disappeared. My brother leapt up and was just on the point of leaving the room when Shao, screaming wildly, came rushing in, saying that he had been visited by apparitions. 'Was it two green men, one big and one little?', asked my brother. 'Nothing of the kind', said Shao. 'When I lay down I at once felt a draught that seemed to come from a small closet close to my bed. It was so ice-cold that my hair stood on end. I was too uncomfortable to sleep, and that was why I went on so long talking to you, though after a time, you did not answer. Presently I saw that in the closet there were about twenty men, some large, some small, with faces round as bowls, moving restlessly about. I made sure it was only my fancy, and took no notice. But suddenly their faces, big and little, appeared at the doorway, in rows, one above the other, till the whole opening was blocked up with faces, the topmost place of all being taken by a huge face as big as a grinding-pan. When all these faces began grinning at me, it was more than I could bear, and throwing aside my pillow I jumped up and came here. But of your "green men" I saw nothing at all.' My brother then told him of what he had seen, and they agreed to leave the place at once, without even getting fodder for their horses. At dawn they heard one groom whisper to another, 'That place we stayed at last night is said to be a ghost-inn. A lot of people who have stayed there have afterwards gone mad, or even died. The officials of the district got tired of having to enquire into all these cases, and more than ten years ago they ordered that the place was to be closed down. If these two gentlemen stayed the night there without coming to any harm, it must either mean that the haunting has ceased, or that the gentlemen are destined by fate to rise high in the world'.

The Chinese, as is generally known, used to call Europeans *fan-kuei*, 'foreign devils'. That, I think, was because the Dutch, English and Russians, with their blond or red hair, reminded them of the devils that figure in Buddhist paintings of Hell. A collection of stories about *kuei* ('devils', 'demons', 'ghosts') would not be complete unless it contained some stories about *fan-kuei*. Yuan's most interesting story of this kind is about Russia. He was told it by his friend Yen Ch'ang-ming (1731–1787), who in turn got it from a Mongol called Umitai, who at the time of the story was a young captain in the Manchu army, but afterwards held many important commands on the north-west frontier. Umitai related that in the Yung Cheng period (1723–1735) he was attached to a mission to Russia. He heard that to the north Russia was bounded by an ocean, and wanted to go and look at it.

The Russians were opposed to this, but he begged so hard to be allowed to, that in the end they gave him an escort of foreigners, who carried compasses and implements for striking a light. For Umitai they provided a carrying-chair with a double lining of felt; his escort rode on camels. After going north for six or seven days they saw a mountain of ice, like a great bastion; so high that its summit was lost in the sky, and shining with so blinding a light that it was not possible to look straight at it. In the base of this mountain was a cave. He crawled into it, guided by his escort, who striking lights and consulting the compass wriggled their way through tortuous passages. After three days they came to the end of the cave and out into a region where the sky was brown, like tortoise-shell. Every now and then a black cloud blew their way, stinging them as though grit had been flung in their faces. The foreigners said it was what was called black hail. They could not bear it for long on end, and every few miles, when they could find a cavern in the rocks, they sheltered there, and started a fire, which they made with saltpetre; for nowhere in that region are there any bushes or trees, nor is there any coal or charcoal. After resting a little they would go on again, and after five or six days they came to two huge bronze figures, facing one another. They were some thirty feet high. One figure rode on a tortoise and the other grasped a serpent in his hand. In front of them was a bronze column with some characters on it in a script that Umitai could not read. The foreigners said that the statues had been erected by the Emperor Yao. They had always heard that what was written on the pillar meant 'Gate into the Cold'. At this point the men of his escort refused to go any further. 'Ahead of us', they said, 'is a sea; but it is still three hundred leagues away. When one gets there, neither the sun nor the stars are visible. The cold is so intense that it cuts one's skin, and if one catches it (i.e. gets frost-bite) one dies. The waters of the sea are black as lead. From time to time these waters part, and out of the rift come ogres and strange beasts, which seize people and carry them away. Even where we are now, water does not flow or fire burn.' To test this last statement Umitai held a lighted torch against his fur coat, and found that, as stated, it did not burn. After a long rest, they started home again. On reaching the town, a roll-call was held, and it was found that out of fifty men, twenty-one had died of frost-bite. Umitai's face was black as pitch and he did not recover his normal complexion for six months. Some of those who went with him had blackened faces for the rest of their days.

Yao, it should be explained, was an ancient Chinese Emperor who thousands of years ago ruled over 'everything under Heaven'. So from a Chinese point of view it was not surprising to find that he had erected a monument in Siberia. The Chinese mission to which Umitai was attached was apparently the one that reached St. Petersburg in 1732. The story seems to be a legendary account of an attempt to explore the White Sea.

The following story is headed, 'It is not always the most reputable people who turn into gods':

A student called Li was going up to Peking for the examinations. At Soochow he hired a launch and had got as far as Huai-an, when there suddenly appeared at the cabin-door a certain Mr. Wang, who had formerly been Li's neighbour. He asked if he might join him. Li consented, and they travelled together for the rest of the day. At nightfall, when they anchored, Wang asked him, with a smile, 'Are you easily frightened?' The question surprised Li. He paused for a moment, and then said, 'I don't think so'. 'I was afraid that I might scare you', said Wang. 'But as you have assured me that you are not easily scared, I had better tell you the truth at once. I am a ghost, not a live man. It is six years since you and I last met. Last year the crops failed, prices soared, and driven by hunger and cold I rifled a tomb, in order to get something valuable to sell for food and firing. But I was arrested, found guilty and executed. And now I am a ghost, hungry and cold as before. I boarded your boat and asked you to take me with you to Peking, because I have a debt to collect there.' 'Who is it that owes you money?', asked Li. 'A certain Mr. Piao', said Wang. 'He is employed by the Board of Punishments, and he promised that when my papers passed through his hands he would erase the death-sentence and substitute something milder, in consideration for which I was to give him five hundred ounces of silver. I managed to collect the sum, but once it was in his hands he ignored his side of the bargain, and the sentence was duly carried out. So now I am going to haunt him.' This Mr. Piao happened to be a relative of Li's. He was very much upset that a member of his family should have behaved in this way. 'The sentence pronounced upon you was of course perfectly in order', he said. 'But my kinsman had no right to rob you in this way. How would it be if I were to take you with me to his house and point out to him how badly he behaved? He would then probably give you your money back and you would no longer feel so bitterly against him. But by the way, as you are dead, I don't quite see what use the money would be to you.' 'It is true that I have not now any use for it,' said Wang, 'but my wife and children are still living quite close to your home, and if we recover the money, I shall ask you to give it to them for me.' Mr. Li promised to do this. Several days later, when they were approaching the Capital, Wang asked leave to go on ahead, saying, 'I'm going off to your relative's house to haunt him. If he has already realized that he is in my power, he is more likely to listen to what you say when you put my case to him. If you were to go there straight away he would certainly take no notice; for he is a man of extremely avaricious disposition'. So saying, Wang disappeared. Li went on into Peking, found himself a lodging, and a few days later went to his kinsman's house. On arriving, he was told that Mr. Piao was suffering from a 'possession'. Shamans, soothsayers, everything had been tried, but all to no purpose. As soon as Li reached the door, the 'possession', speaking through the sick man's mouth, shouted out, 'Now's your chance, people! Your star of deliverance has arrived'. The people of the house all rushed out to meet Li, asking him what the madman's words meant. Li told them the whole story, and Piao's wife at first suggested burning a considerable quantity of paper money in payment of the debt. At this the sick man roared with laughter. 'Pay back real money with make-believe money!', he said. 'Nothing in this world can be disposed of quite so conveniently as that! Count out five hundred ounces of silver at once, and hand them over to our friend here. I shan't let go of you till you do.' The Piaos produced the money, and Mr. Piao at once recovered his senses.

Some days later the ghost turned up at Li's lodging and urged him to set out for the South at once. 'But I have not sat for my examination yet', said Li. 'You are not going to pass,' said the ghost, 'so there is no point in sitting.' Li, however, insisted on remaining at Peking. After he had sat for the examination, the ghost again urged him to start for home. 'Do let me just wait till the results are out', said Li. 'You haven't passed,' said the ghost, 'so what is the point of waiting for the results?' When the results were published, Li's name was not on the list. 'Now perhaps you'll consent to start', said the ghost, laughing. Ashamed of having kept him waiting for nothing, Li agreed to start immediately. On the boat he noticed that Wang sniffed at things to eat and drink, but never swallowed them, and that if he sniffed at anything hot, it at once became icy-cold. When they got to Sutsien, the ghost said, 'They are giving a play in that village over there. Let's go and look on'. When they had watched several episodes, the ghost suddenly disappeared. But Li heard somewhere nearby a

> sound of sand flying and pebbles rolling. He thought he had better go to the boat and wait till the ghost came back. It was getting dark when the ghost at last reappeared, dressed up very grandly. 'Good-bye,' he said, 'I'm staying here. I've got the job of being the God of War.' 'How have you managed that?', asked Li, very much surprised. 'All the so-called Goddesses of Mercy and Gods of War down here in this world are merely ghosts passing themselves off as divinities. The play we saw was given in pursuance of a vow to the God of War. But the local "God of War" is in fact the ghost of a scamp who did far worse things than I ever did. I suddenly made up my mind I would oust him from his job, so I went and had a scuffle with him and drove him away. I dare say you heard the noise of sand flying and pebbles rolling.' With these words, the ghost bowed his thanks and vanished. Li went on down the Canal, and eventually handed over the five hundred ounces of silver to the ghost's family.

Many of the stories are about members of Yuan Mei's own family. The following anecdote about his grandmother's grandmother must take us well back into the Ming dynasty:

> My grandmother Ch'ai once told me that her maternal grandmother Yang, being old and childless, went and lived with my aunt Mrs. Hung, and died in her house at the great age of ninety-six. She lived in an upper room, where she spent her time worshipping Buddha and reciting the Scriptures. For thirty years she never set foot on the ground floor. She was very tender-hearted, and if she heard the sound of some man-servant or maid-servant being beaten downstairs, she got into such a state of agitation that she could not eat. If any servants came up to her room, she always shared her food with them. After she reached the age of ninety, whenever she bowed to Buddha, the Buddha image she had in her room stood up and bowed to her. This terrified her, and she used to make my grandmother, who

was still only a child, come and sit with her. 'When you are here,' she said, 'Buddha does not bow back at me'.

Three days before she died she asked for a tub to wash her feet in. The maid brought her the wooden tub that she always used. 'Not that one', she said. 'Where I am going now my feet will be resting on the Lotus Flower. You must bring me the bronze ewer that I wash my face in.' When the ewer arrived, a fragrance of sandal-wood suddenly came down out of the sky and filled every corner of the room. She sat upright with her legs crossed, and died. The fragrance lingered in her room for three whole nights and days.

Those who are reincarnated in the Paradise of Amitabha are given lotus flowers to stand on. The piety of one's grandmother's grandmother is all very well. But an excess of piety in one's own household may be exasperating:

My concubine Miss Fang worshipped a small sandal-wood image of Kuan-yin, four inches high. I am by nature very tolerant. I did not join her in her performances; but I did not forbid them. An old servant called Mrs. Chang worshipped this same image with great devotion and would never begin her house-work in the morning till she had gone and burnt incense in front of it and bowed her head. I happened one day to get up earlier than usual. I called out to Mrs. Chang to bring my hot water immediately for washing my face in. But she had not finished her prostrations, and took no notice. I was so angry that I took the image, flung it on the floor and kicked it. Miss Fang, my concubine, heard of this, and said weeping, 'Last night I dreamt that Kuan-yin came to say good-bye to me. "Tomorrow", she said, "there is going to be a wicked assault upon me, and I shall not be able to stay here." Now you have kicked her, which is certainly the fulfilment of my dream.' She then took the image to be looked after at the Cundi Shrine. I thought to myself 'Buddhism is an abstract philosophy. It

> does not deal in prophecy or clever tricks of that kind. Some evil spirit must certainly have "possessed" the image'. After that I never allowed my household to worship Buddhas.

It is strange to find one of the most easy-going and sceptical men of his generation behaving on this occasion in so tyrannical and at the same time so superstitious a way.

A story about the ghost of Chiang T'ing-hsi (1669–1732) well illustrates the 'clash of generations'. The men of the early eighteenth century were on the whole stern and puritanical, those of the mid-century pleasure-loving and tolerant, those of its closing years and the early nineteenth century, once more straightlaced and censorious. The father of Yuan Mei's examiner Chiang P'u was a typical scholar of the old, severe school.

> He warned his sons and grandsons against ever having anything to do with actors, and as long as he was alive no actor or entertainer ever came near the house. When he had been dead for ten years (i.e. in 1742) Chiang P'u began occasionally to get actors from outside to give performances. But he still did not venture to keep a private troupe in the house. An old family servant called Ku Sheng, when chatting one day with Chiang P'u, got on to the subject of theatricals. 'A company of actors from outside', he pleaded, 'is never so good as a troupe trained in the house, or so handy. A lot of the servants here have children. Why don't you get hold of a teacher, make him select the likeliest and have them trained as a company?' Chiang P'u was much attracted by the idea; but before he could answer he suddenly saw that Ku Sheng's face was transfigured by a look of abject terror. He held his two hands in front of him as though to receive handcuffs, and fell prostrate on the ground. Then he inserted his head between the legs of the table and worked his way from one table-leg to another till the table completely covered him, like the lid of a box.

Chiang called to him, but he did not answer. He then sent urgent messages to shamans and doctors; but nothing they could do was of any avail. However, at midnight he began to revive and was able at last to say, 'What a fright I have had, what a fright! Just after my last remark to you, a huge figure appeared and dragged me off to a hall in which my old master was sitting. Looking at me reproachfully my master said in a stern voice, "I am surprised that you, who have been in the service of my family from generation to generation, should ignore my last wishes and persuade Wu-lang (Chiang P'u's intimate name) to keep actors". He then had me bound; I was given forty strokes with the rod and shut up alive in a coffin. I was completely stupefied, and did not know what to do. At last I heard voices calling to me and, still lying in my coffin, I tried to answer, but could not. After a time, however, I began to feel less confused; but I still did not know how to get out'. They looked at his back and saw there actually were blue-black weals on it.

A number of stories concern planchette-seances. The planchette does not seem to have been used in early China; but from the eleventh century A.D. onwards it is constantly mentioned. Seances were of two kinds. They were held by Taoist priests in temples, in order to get into touch with the presiding deity. In such cases sand was spread on the temple-altar, and the marks on the sand were made by a stylus suspended from a sort of small gallows. Two priests, standing back to back, rested their hands on the 'gallows'. More commonly Yuan Mei's stories deal with seances conducted at private houses. At these, the sand was spread on a flat dish or tray. Sometimes such gatherings took the whole business very seriously; sometimes it was treated chiefly as an opportunity for witticisms at the expense of the control-spirit (*chi hsien*) who was supposed to have 'possessed' the planchette. Many controls (as also at Western seances) claimed to be the spirits of illustrious ancient persons or at any rate to be on terms of intimacy with such persons in the Realms of the Dead, and to be able to obtain information from them. The controls, however, were naturally apt to give themselves away by making historical blunders, and it was awkward for them if anyone present was learned enough to check up on their information.

Yuan Mei does not rule out the possibility that the two people whose hands rested on the apparatus might occasionally conspire to 'fake' communications. But he seems to have believed that in general disembodied spirits did actually 'possess' the planchette. He had, however, a low opinion of the verses they wrote, as also of their general education. He tells us of a control who claimed to be the author of the tomb-inscription of Chang Hsi-ku (A.D. 683–754). A learned person who was present pointed out to the control that the inscription mentions a militia-headquarters which is unknown to the *History of the T'ang Dynasty*. The control was evidently put out by this and for a while the planchette stopped. But presently it moved again, and the control promised to come back next day after having ascertained from the author of the History (a famous eleventh-century writer) why he had ignored the existence of this regiment. The promise, however, was not kept; and in future whenever this learned gentleman was present, the control failed to turn up.

This is, of course, only an anecdote, not a piece of historical research. But to make it effective it was essential to get the facts right, which Yuan Mei fails to do. The person who the ghost claimed to be was not, as Yuan and the ghost supposed, the author of the inscription, but merely the calligrapher from whose fair copy the inscription was cut. The ghost, had it known this, was therefore in a position to disclaim all responsibility for statements made in the inscription. The story is clearly intended to make fun of a pretentious control, and at the same time to show Yuan's scholarly acumen. In fact, however, it chiefly illustrates the rather slipshod nature of his antiquarian studies.

There are several very odd stories about the habits of foreigners.

> In the country of the Red Haired People (i.e. the Dutch or English) there is a great deal of going with singing-girls. The customers set out wine and send for a girl. They rip off her under-clothes, gather round her and spit into her person. They do not demand any greater intimacy. When they have finished spitting, they send her away. To reward her they call on everyone to put money in a bag.

Another odd piece of information is headed 'The Siamese have a donkey as wife'. 'The Siamese are very lustful folk. When a boy is fourteen or fifteen his parents find him a she-ass to be his wife. At night when he is asleep they tie the ass by his bed and put his male organ into the ass's female one. They think this makes him grow up particularly strong and healthy. After three years he marries a proper, human wife; but he keeps the she-ass for the rest of its existence, treating it as a secondary wife. No girl will consent to marry any man who has not first had a donkey as his wife.'

Oddly enough in the separate editions of the *Tzu Pu Yü* (as opposed to the version included in the complete Works) this story is told not of the Siamese, but of the Moslems (*Hui-hui*). I imagine that 'Moslems' was what originally stood in the text, but that someone with knowledge of the Moslems in Turkestan questioned the truth of the story, and Yuan Mei transferred it to Siam which, unlike Turkestan, was not part of the Chinese Empire.

Sir George Staunton in his account of Lord Macartney's embassy to China tells us that there was a great demand there for 'pieces of complicated mechanism producing, by means of internal springs and wheels, movements apparently spontaneous.' 'These', he says, 'were in pidgin English called "sing-songs".' Yuan Mei tells us that

> in the twenty-ninth year of Ch'ien Lung (1764) the people of the Western Ocean (i.e. Europeans) sent as tribute a

troupe of eighteen actors, made of metal, who could act part of *The Western Pavilion*. The actors were about a foot high. Their bodies, ears, eyes, hands and feet were all cast in bronze. Their hearts, bellies, kidneys and intestines were all linked up by a secret mechanism, like the works of a self-chiming clock. For each fresh episode a key had to be inserted to open the lock. The adjustment had to be absolutely correct; if the lock was wrongly opened, the sitting, lying, walking and stopping of the figures were all awry. The hero, Chang; his beloved, Ying-ying; her maid, Hung-niang, and the monks Hui-ming and Fa-tsung could all walk about by themselves, open doors, and put on their clothes. They bore themselves, met, greeted, came forward, retreated and so on exactly like real people. The only disappointment was that they could not sing. When an episode was over, they undressed themselves and lay down flat in their box. When it was time to act again, they got up unaided and went back on to their stage. Such is the consummate skill of the men of the Western Ocean!

The play in question has been translated into English by Mr. Hsiung, the author of the play *Lady Precious Stream*, and is one of the few Chinese plays that is fairly well known to Western readers.

Sir Aurel Stein, the discoverer of the famous Caves of the Thousand Buddhas at Tun-huang in the extreme west of China, spent some days at another group of caves not far from Tun-huang, called the Gorge (or Cliff) of the Myriad Buddhas (*Wan Fo Hsia*). He describes this group in Volume III of *Serindia* and says it would be interesting to find some mention of it in Chinese sources. This is what Yuan Mei says of it:

In the fiftieth year of K'ang Hsi (1711) a voice suddenly called down from the top of the Ho-li Mountain in Kansu province saying 'Open, or not open?', 'Open, or not open?' This went on for several days; but no one dared to reply.

One day a shepherd boy passed that way, and for fun answered, 'Open!' A moment later there was a loud rending noise, a rush of wind and a clap of thunder. The rock of the mountain-side burst wide open, disclosing a cliff covered with thousands of images of Bodhisattvas, all natural, not made by hand. Even their hair and eyebrows were all complete. People still call it the Cliff of the Myriad Buddhas. The Commissioner Chang Fan-kuei passed by this place and saw these images with his own eyes.

One of the grottoes has been excellently described and illustrated by Langdon Warner in his 'Buddhist Wall-paintings. A study of a ninth-century grotto at Wan Fo Hsia', published in 1938. Chinese writers in the eighteenth century were not much interested in Buddhist sites. The Gazetteer of Kansu Province (A.D. 1736) has only four or five lines even about the Tun-huang caves, and does not mention the Cliff of the Myriad Buddhas at all. Indeed, Yuan Mei's piece of folklore may be the only reference to the Cliff that exists in Chinese literature prior to the twentieth century. His informant, Chang Fan-kuei (1736–1803), a fervent Buddhist and author of a commentary on the *Heart Sutra* was more likely than an orthodox Confucian to take an interest in works of Buddhist art. He was Prefect of Wei-yuan in Kansu in 1764, and it was presumably about then that he saw the Wan Fo Hsia grottoes.

Another whole class of stories concerns ingenious frauds, confidence-tricks and so on. Here is one of them:

A man who was wearing new shoes was walking through the market-place when he was accosted by someone who bowed low, grasped his hand and began chatting to him. The wearer of the shoes was puzzled and said, 'I don't think we have ever met before'. 'Oho', said the other, 'you think because you are wearing new shoes that you are entitled to forget your old friends!' And so saying, he seized the first man's hat, threw it up on to a neighbouring roof, and ran off. The man with the shoes made sure that the fellow had been drinking, and that this was just a drunken prank. While he was hesitating what to do next, another man came along, and said, 'That was a low trick the fellow played upon you, wasn't it? But you must not stand with the sun pouring on to your bare head. You hád better go up on to the roof and get your hat.' 'I should need a ladder', said the man with the shoes. 'I'm a bit of an acrobat', said the other. 'You can use my shoulder as a ladder, and get up that way if you like.' The man with the shoes thanked him warmly. The second man then knelt on the ground, let the other put his feet on his shoulders, and reared himself up. When the man with the shoes had almost reached the level of the roof, the other said crossly: 'Do be a bit less inconsiderate! I mind about my shirt just as much as you mind about your hat. Your shoes may be new, but the soles are pretty muddy all the same. It doesn't seem to occur to you that you're making a mess of the shoulders of my shirt.' The man apologized profusely, took off his shoes, handed them to the other and standing on his shoulders with only his socks on his feet, reached the top. Meanwhile the other ran off with his shoes. The first man had now recovered his hat, but he was up on the roof, with no way of getting down. Passers-by imagined that the two were old friends who were having a game with one another, and did not offer him assistance. Only when he had shouted desperate appeals for some time did a neighbour find a ladder and get him down. By then the man who ran off with the shoes had, of course, completely disappeared.

A story which Yuan obviously concocted to express his own views is contained in the Supplement to the collection. It is about a man who 'died and came to life again'. He was surprised when he reached the Nether Regions to find a woman from his own village, who was a notorious adulteress, being launched on to a very high-class new incarnation, instead of being (as he would have expected) detained in Hell for punishment. 'Oh, that's not at all the sort of thing they worry about here', the people in the Land of the Dead explained. 'King Yama (the king of the Dead) is a dignified, straight-forward deity. One can't imagine him hiding under people's beds and spying upon what they do together in private.'

I will finish these extracts with an anecdote (also from the Supplement) which I am afraid some readers may think rather trivial:

> A monk of the Wu-t'ai Shan had a disciple who came to him when he was only two years old. They lived on the very top of the mountain, pursuing their devotions, and for ten years never once went down into the plain. When at last they one day came down to the nearest village, the boy saw many things he had never seen before. The Master was obliged to explain, 'This is an ox; it is used when one is ploughing a field. This is a horse; it is used for riding on. This is a cock; it announces the dawn. This is a dog; he guards the gate', and so on. After a time, they met a girl. 'What is that?', asked the disciple. 'That is a tiger', said the monk, afraid that the boy might take a fancy to her. 'If anyone goes near it, the creature devours him, bones and all.'
>
> That evening, when they were back on the mountain, the monk said, 'What did you think of all the things we saw today? Was there anything you took a fancy to?' 'I keep on thinking of that man-eating tiger we met', the boy said. 'I can't get the creature out of my head.'

It may be thought that as most of the stories in Yuan Mei's ghost-book were told to him by friends, they have little relevance to his own work as a creative writer and ought not to occupy so large a space in my account of him. But we may assume, I think, that he treated his material with considerable freedom. His old friend the dramatist Yang Ch'ao-kuan, who like Yuan Mei had been a protégé of the Manchu grandee

Ortai, appears to have told him, in 1770, that when he was acting as examiner in 1752, his attention had been called to the merits of a certain candidate by a beautiful lady, who appeared to him in a dream. He was amazed to discover, when he read Yuan Mei's book, that the lady of his dream had been turned into the ghost of Li Hsiang-chün, the most famous courtesan of the seventeenth century. 'Mr. Yang', he read, 'went about everywhere boasting that he had seen Li Hsiang-chün', which was rather as though you or I were to pride ourselves on having seen Nell Gwynne. In an angry letter Yang protested against this falsification. 'I am not at all averse to gallantry,' he wrote, 'but I am not in the least attracted by loose women or singing-girls. . . . What I saw in my dream was the ghost of a respectable woman.' He also (rather pedantically) corrects a number of small mistakes in Yuan Mei's account; for example, there were seventy-one not eighty-three candidates at the examination! He winds up, as one would expect, by condemning the title (*What the Master did not talk of*) as 'a clear blasphemy against the Sage'. Yuan Mei in his reply says that if Yang refuses to make love to disreputable women, his only alternative is to court respectable ones, 'a course which is likely to get you into serious trouble'. He also insists (and he may really have thought so) that he had put down the story exactly as Yang told it. 'After all, it was your dream, not mine,' Yuan says, 'and if you had not told it to me, I should have known nothing about this weighty matter at all.' It was not the first time that these two old friends found themselves in disagreement. 'We had been friends since boyhood,' writes Yuan Mei in his biographical sketch of Yang Ch'ao-kuan, 'but in temperament two boys could hardly have been more different. I was rash; he was timid. I was a careless genius; he was solid and serious. I had no taste for Taoism and Buddhism; he was passionately devoted to Zen, and towards the end of his life kept vows of abstinence very strictly. So we had plenty of things to disagree about. But all the same when he was Governor of Chiung-chou (in Szechwan) he sent me 300 ounces of silver, asking me to take him a house in Nanking, in order that he spend his old age near to me.'

A collection of somewhat similar stories, the *Liao Chai Chih I*, is familiar to English readers owing to the fact that about a third of it was translated by Professor H. A. Giles in 1908, under the title *Strange Stories from a Chinese Studio*, a book which has had a wide circulation and has been several times reprinted. The author of the *Strange Stories*, P'u Sung-ling (1640–1715) was little known in his own day, and the stories were not printed till 1766. There is no evidence that Yuan Mei knew the *Liao Chai Chih I*, and though the subject-matter of his 'ghost stories' is often similar, in style they are very different; P'u Sung-ling's book being in allusive, elaborately poetic language, whereas Yuan Mei's is in the simplest and most direct style.

CHAPTER SIX

Journeys

IN 1781 Yuan Mei had arranged with his Buddhist friend Hsiang Yung to go with him on a tour to the famous Buddhist site, T'ien-t'ai, which is about 200 miles south-east of Nanking. Hsiang Yung, it will be remembered, was one of the friends who tried to persuade him to study the *Śūrangama Sūtra*. He was fond of religious discussions, and seems to have been a very serious character. For some reason the plan fell through, and Yuan arranged instead to take as his companion a young man of about twenty called Liu Chih-p'eng. Liu had taken his First Degree at the age of fifteen. He was cultivated and intelligent, wrote poetry and painted a little, orchids being his speciality. But he was fonder of amusement than of books, and spent much of his time with the singing-girls on the boat-houses along the Ch'in-huai Canal. He was a descendant of Liu Tsung-chou (1578–1645), patriot, scholar and philosopher, who starved himself to death rather than witness the triumph of the Manchus, when Nanking fell in 1645. This great ancestor wrote a number of short tracts, in a clear and easy style, on moral defects and how to cure them. They were founded on the lectures he gave at the Chi-shan Academy at Shao-hsing, and were used as school-texts for long afterwards. Among the offences against which he warned his pupils were 'taking a concubine without due cause', 'bringing singing-girls to the house', 'excessive affection for wife and children', 'composing songs', 'going to the theatre', 'love of antiques, or of calligraphy and paintings', 'listening to one's wife's advice', 'bowing to monks or nuns'. There is also a warning against reading a passage here and there in books, instead of reading from cover to cover. Apropos of this last injunction, I remember that my father's old governess, Miss Keeling, thought it wicked not to finish a book she had begun, and consequently felt obliged, if she picked up by mistake some desperately technical work on economics that my father had left lying about, to read it through to the bitter end. Liu Tsung-chou's frivolous descendant must often have been twitted by his elders for failing so signally to live up to the precepts of his famous ancestor.

It was on the eighteenth day of the tenth month of 1780 that Yuan and Liu Chih-p'eng first met, and Yuan cherished the date, for years to come, as a sentimental anniversary. Liu was very good-looking, and when he and Yuan went boating together everyone on the banks turned round and stared at the boat. Yuan Mei fondly imagined, writes his friend Chao I, that they were staring in wonder and awe at the greatest poet of the day; but in reality they were looking at his remarkably handsome young friend, whom Chao I (by a rather sinister allusion) compares to an ancient prodigy of male beauty called Wei Chieh, who was 'stared to death' at the age of twenty-six.

The journey began with a visit to his daughter at Li-yang where, it will be remembered, she had recently married a grandson of Yuan Mei's old patron Shih I-chih. The young man was living with his father Shih I-ang (1712–1791) who after having a row with his superiors at the Board of War, had for sixteen years been living in retirement at Li-yang. Shih I-chih, Yuan's devoted patron, had died in 1763, and his house had now become a sort of mausoleum. Here were treasured the poems addressed to him and the patents conferred upon him by successive Emperors, a set of the Great Encyclopedia (first printed in 1728), presented to him by the Emperor Yung Cheng, a silver cup commemorating his Governor-Generalship of Kiangnan and Kiangsi in 1730, and a picture of his wedding procession, in which he figured on horseback.

Yuan Mei also, of course, visited his patron's tomb. When he was first introduced to the great man at Peking in 1739, Shih I-chih had exclaimed, 'How young you are!'; and in the poem Yuan now wrote he said, 'I know that you in the grave below once more will be surprised—not at "how young" I am, but at how grey I have grown'.

A few days before Yuan's arrival his daughter had given birth to a son, and the visit was no doubt timed in connection with this event.

Proceeding on their journey, about seventeen miles north of T'ien-t'ai, they came to a village called 'Stripy Bamboos'. 'It is surrounded', writes Yuan Mei, 'by high hills and boisterous waterfalls. There are over twenty "houses with green upper-storeys", built against the side of the hill. They seemed to be chiefly inhabited by a bevy of young girls, who were now, with mountain flowers stuck in their hair, washing clothes by the stream-side. We sat on a rock by the stream and talked to them. They were not in the least shy, but were also not at all coquettish. They were in fact singularly fresh, agreeable young people. When their bright combs and hairpins flashed against the grey clouds they did really look more like fairies than human beings.' Liu (his young companion) took a fancy to a girl called Chiang and stayed the night with her. 'But before dawn he turned up where I was lodging, with his clothes thrown loosely over his shoulders, complaining that the noise of the waterfalls all round prevented him from sleeping.'

'Houses with green upper-storeys' usually means brothels, and the village seems to have been a sort of rural *quartier-libre*, patronized perhaps chiefly by pilgrims on their way to the holy places of the T'ien-t'ai.

On the T'ien-t'ai mountains he met a monk called Li-chung, a man of over seventy, who said he came from Nanking and told many stories of the time when Yuan Mei was Prefect there, 'while all the other monks sat round in a circle, bowing low'.

Who could have supposed that all these things of forty years ago
Would be told to me by an old monk on the rugged mountain-side?
His information is not perhaps complete in every detail;
If it were, there might be items unsuited to this occasion!

Whenever he came to a monastery, the monks would come out in a body to welcome him. 'They beat their gongs and drums', he says, 'and requested me to bow to the Buddha. On one such occasion I improvised the following quatrain and wrote it on a fan, that they might understand my point of view':

When I meet a monk, I never fail to greet him;
When I see a Buddha I do not bow down.
If one bows to a Buddha, the Buddha does not know;
If one greets a monk, one is greeting what is actually there.

His friend Wang Wen-chih (who had become a Buddhist lay-brother in 1778) heard of this epigram, and said, 'You do not like Buddha; but in what you say I often see the influence of Buddhist ideas'. Near T'ien-t'ai he visited the brothers of Ch'i Shao-nan, who were still living at the small farm that was left to the family when Ch'i Shao-nan got into trouble with the Literary Inquisition in 1768 and, as we have seen (p. 100), the considerable estates of the Ch'i family were confiscated. They asked him to go through their brother's works, cut out anything indiscreet and write a preface to them. Yuan Mei spent all night in doing so, and this was a courageous act, considering that it was because of a preface that Ch'i Shao-nan himself had got into trouble. Works by Ch'i would in any case be considered suspect, and however carefully Yuan Mei went through them, it was always possible that the authorities might find a hidden meaning in some apparently harmless phrase. This was perhaps the collection that was ultimately printed in 1797.

At Rainbow Bridge, on the way to Wen-chou, in the extreme south of Kiangsu Province, 'we stayed with a Mr. Ni. His children's tutor, a Mr. Chang, asked to be presented to me. He seemed very full of himself, and when he was brought along took no notice of me at all, but began boasting about the celebrity of his father who, he said, had been on extremely intimate terms with Yuan Mei and Shang P'an. "Did you ever see this person Yuan, about whom you are talking?", I asked him. "Oh, he lived a long time ago", said the tutor. "I doubt if he is still alive; if he is, he must be in his dotage by now. I'm far too young ever to have seen him." "He's here in front of you", I said. This was a shock for Mr. Chang, who at once prostrated himself before me'.

Being both of them poets, Yuan Mei and his young companion could not omit Yung-chia, near Wen-chou, from their itinerary; for it was here that the famous poet Hsieh Ling-yun (A.D. 385–433) was once Governor. The entry to the town was by a river so narrow that the eaves of the houses on either bank almost met; and so low were these eaves that one had to duck one's head to avoid them, 'just as out of respect one lowers one's head when one passes through the gate of some great man's residence; though these were in fact very humble dwellings'. On a rock at Yung-chia were shown marks supposed to have been made by the nails of the special climbing-shoes invented by Hsieh Ling-yun, who was a great mountaineer; and on a cliff there was an inscription in archaic writing supposed to have been carved by him. There was too a portrait of Hsieh Ling-yun, in which he looked so inspired that 'one could almost hear verses coming out of his mouth'. Hsieh had remarkably fine moustaches and it is said that when about to be executed in 433 he cut them off and presented them to a monastery, that they might adorn an image of Vimalakīrti. When early in the eighth century the Princess An-lo was playing the 'Contest of the Hundred Herbs', a game of chance always played on the fifth day of the fifth month, she sent to the monastery for Hsieh's moustaches, to serve as a stake in the game. But in the picture, says Yuan Mei, his long moustaches are eternally intact. He cannot give them away; nor can a Princess commandeer them as a gambling stake.

Having heard that in the neighbourhood of Wen-chou there were very curious wedding-customs, they went to a wedding. 'On the third day after the marriage the bridegroom's family give a wine-feast, with music. They invite all the handsomest women in the district and seat them in two rows. The bride sits with her face to the south. The doors of the house are flung wide open, and anyone who likes can come and look on. The ladies show no sign of embarrassment. If anyone takes a fancy to one of the ladies in the two rows (those to the east being married women and those to the west, unmarried girls) he walks straight up to her and hands her a drink. She then salutes him in return, drinks the wine and again bows to the stranger.

'On this occasion the girl who was third in the row of unmarried women was remarkably handsome. I am no hand at wine-drinking and did not venture to toast her. But my friend Liu Chih-p'eng gaily saluted her and poured out a cup. She rose to her feet and performed a double prostration. When she had drunk the cup he had offered, she poured out one for him, but absent-mindedly began to drink it herself. The master of ceremonies called out to her, "That is your admirer's wine!" The girl was evidently much embarrassed; but with a captivating smile she at once handed the cup to Liu, who plainly thought it an honour to be favoured with the dregs of this handsome girl's wine.' In another account of this episode Yuan Mei says that a long interchange of drinks between these beauties and their admirers is thought to ensure a numerous posterity in the family; so that only visitors with a great capacity for drinking venture to come forward. 'Mr. Cheng, the Governor of the place,' Yuan continues, 'considered the custom contrary to the Rites and was proposing to put a stop to it. But I said to him, "If it is a question of the Rites, then they must be carried out properly; but if it is a mere question of usage, then local customs should be followed. They are what are called 'The Rites of those who have no Rites'".' Yuan then composed a series of poems describing the wedding, and the Governor said laughing: 'For the present I shall not interfere with this vulgar custom. The fact that it has supplied you with a subject for a set of poems is sufficient excuse for it.'

In and around Wen-chou a very peculiar dialect is spoken: 'There are many very pretty girls; but unfortunately one cannot understand what they say. We came across some particularly attractive ones who were chatting together while they wove rattan trays; but we could not understand a word they said.' Small wonder that they could not understand; the word 'tray', for example, in ordinary Chinese *p'an*, is pronounced *bo* at Wen-chou. 'What an advantage it would be', Yuan Mei observes, 'if interpreters were stationed in Paradises such as this, so that the devotees of these divinities might be able to communicate their sentiments.'

In the Yen-tang range nearby they visited the Cave of Kuan-yin: 'It is very high and spacious, and there is room in it for a thousand people. To reach it one has to clamber up a rock-causeway of 377 steps. I hired a strong man to help me up. It is said that in the thirtieth year of Chia-ching (1551) the Inspector Liu Yun-sheng and his two daughters became Immortals in this place. There are very fine stucco figures of them. I stayed in the cave for a long time, and at last going down the steps continually paused and looked back with longing, improvising while I did so the poem:

An ageing man I leave the Immortals' Cave;
Down and down, with a halt at every step.
For I know in my heart that once I leave this place
It is quite certain I shall never come again.'

The travellers now turned inland and near Ch'u-chou, about fifty miles north-west of Wen-chou, Yuan wrote a long poem on his misplaced sympathy for the sturdy chair-men who had carried him over hill and dale:

Today my carriers have had a double task;
We have gone up a mountain and then down into a valley.

For the moment they are through with all their hardships and dangers;
Night is falling, and at last they can rest their feet.
I was quite certain that directly they put down their burden
Tired out, they would sink into a heavy sleep.
To my great surprise they re-trimmed the lamp
And all night long played at games of chance.
A quarrel began; feeling ran high.
One of them absconded; another went in chase.
All the fuss was about a handful of pence;
Hardly enough to pay for a cup of gruel.
Yet they throw down those pence with as high and mighty an air
As if they were flinging a shower of golden stars.
Next day when they shouldered their burdens again
Their strength was greater that that of Pen and Yü.
The same thing happened five nights on end;
It was almost as if some demon had possessed them.
Can it be, I wonder, that when the dice are thrown
The Owl and the Black have the power to cure fatigue?
But different creatures have their different natures;
What suits the fish will not please the bear.
The simplest folk and the most learned men
Cannot possibly be measured by the same rules.
Rather than sorrow over other people's sorrows
It is better, when one can, to enjoy one's own pleasures.

The Owl and the Black, it should be explained, were the names of dice-throws.

Having arranged to stay for the night at an inn near Ch'u-chou, Yuan Mei went for a little walk and noticed a tiled (that is to say, an upper-class) house. He strolled towards it, had a few words with the owner, a Mr. Yü, and came back to the inn. 'I was just about to undress and go to bed, when I heard voices outside the door, and going to see who was there, I found it was Mr. Yü, who had only just read the visiting-card I had given him, and six or seven of his brothers. "You can't surely be the great Yuan Mei?", he said. When I affirmed that I was, he looked me up and down by the light of the lantern he was carrying. "We have all of us read your collection of examination essays," he said, "but we thought you lived at the beginning of the Manchu dynasty. You don't look much over sixty. You must surely be the ancient Yuan Mei come back to life! But you must not go off again at once. I should like to show you the sights of the neighbourhood. You must let us take you up the Hsien-tu Peak." At once some members of his party took down my bed-hangings, while others rolled up my mats. His servants shouldered my luggage and took me in a carrying-chair to his house, where he entertained me magnificently. The next day we went on horseback up the Peak.'

'When we were crossing the Orchid Stream (Lan-ch'i) someone told us that from there to Wu-i (the Bohea of Europeans) was only a matter of ten days, and urged us to make this detour. But the weather was now becoming so hot that I was in a hurry to get home. Afterwards, however, it got cooler, and I was sorry we did not take this advice.' They were back again in Nanking on the 27th of the fifth month.

'When Liu Chih-p'eng first came to see me he gave me about a dozen of his poems. Not wishing to seem ungrateful, I pasted them all up on the wall, which evidently pleased him. Afterwards when we went to T'ien-t'ai together, we exchanged poems the whole time; but neither of us mentioned the poems he had given me before. When he got back to Nanking, after having been away for about two months, he rushed straight to my house, tore down his poems from the wall and burnt them. He then turned to me and laughed uproariously. "A fine fellow after all, a fine fellow!", I said.'

Soon after his return Yuan Mei received a letter from his old friend Shen Jung-ch'ang (now over seventy), warning him against continuing, at the age of sixty-six, to 'seek the Spring', that is to say, indulge in love-affairs. Jung-ch'ang himself, though he had passed the normal retiring age, had just gone to

Peking to put in for a job. Yuan Mei replied with the following poem:

A certain person regardless of his age
Has gone to the City to get himself a job.
Another person regardless of his age
When he looks at 'flowers' from time to time succumbs.
Between the failings of these two men there is not anything to choose;
The two shepherds Tsang and Ku both lost their sheep.
Some insects eat sugar, some prefer nettles.
Let us each find pleasure where we can, and not chide one another!

The first stanza, it will be noticed, is in five-syllable metre; the second in seven-syllable. The line about the two shepherds is an allusion to a passage in Chapter VIII of *Chuang Tzu*: The two shepherds Tsang and Ku both lost their sheep. It was found that Tsang lost his while reading a book; Ku had been playing at dice. 'In their preoccupations they were different; but in the fact that they lost their sheep they were the same.'

Among the many people who called on Yuan Mei when he was away at T'ien-t'ai was the poet and painter T'ung Yü (1721–1782), 'the friend whom I never met'. T'ung lived about forty-five miles south-east of Hangchow. He never went in for the examinations or held any official post, but devoted himself entirely to writing and painting. Yuan Mei first met with his poems in 1756 and immensely admired them. He heard that T'ung Yü reciprocated the feeling and regarded him as the greatest poet of the day. Years passed without their meeting, and when Yuan passed through T'ung's home-town in 1782, on his way to the T'ien-t'ai, T'ung was away. He was in fact at Yangchow. He made an excursion to Nanking, in the hope of seeing Yuan Mei; only to find that Yuan was at the T'ien-t'ai! Later in the year, when he heard that Yuan was back at Nanking he wrote proposing to come there and visit him. But Yuan was then intending to go to Yangchow and fearing that they might again miss one another in the same provoking way as in the spring, wrote urging T'ung to stay where he was. Various unexpected circumstances delayed Yuan's visit to Yangchow and when he at last arrived on the 13th of the tenth month, he found that T'ung Yü had died ten days before. 'It was a great joy to my father', T'ung's son told him, 'to know that you were coming, and during his illness, whenever there was a knock at the door, he said, "I expect that is Mr. Yuan". The day before he died, he said, "The only thing that is worrying me is that it does not look as though I were going to see Mr. Yuan after all".' At the invitation of the family Yuan Mei took part in the ritual lamentations, wrote the tomb-inscription and also wrote a preface to T'ung Yü's collected poems. During his last illness T'ung had painted a plum-tree branch, meaning to present the picture to Yuan, but died before he had put in the blossoms. Yuan took back the unfinished painting to Nanking and treasured it for the rest of his life.

Yuan Mei's great detractor, Chang Hsueh-ch'eng (see above, p. 101) asserted some fifteen years later that a quiet and orderly man like T'ung Yü could not possibly ever have had dealings of any kind with a low debauchee such as Yuan Mei!

In the spring of 1783 Yuan's young friend Liu got married, borrowing for the occasion a brocade bed-spread from Yuan. But a month later he carried Liu off for an excursion to the Huang-shan (Yellow Mountains), about fifty miles south-west of Nanking, on the far side of the Yangtze. At one point they came to a dark cleft called the Bottomless Ravine. 'I dangled one foot a few inches over the side. The monk (from the Lion Forest Monastery) who was with us was terrified and dragged me back. "It wouldn't have mattered if I had fallen in", I said, laughing. "What do you mean?", he asked. "Well," I said, "if it is really bottomless, I should have gone on fluttering harmlessly down for ever. But if there is a bottom I must eventually have arrived at it, and in the end someone would have come to my rescue." We had not any rope with us; but I tied a piece of iron to a string, and let it down. The chasm turned out to be only a few feet deep! The monk roared with laughter.'

During the Huang-shan trip their enjoyment was often spoilt by clouds and mist:

Down in the valley it is pleasant to look at clouds;
But up on the mountain to get into cloud is dismal.
All of a sudden those dense vapours come;
At the same instant every eye is blind.
They did not come here for the purpose of making rain;
They only came to plunge us in chaotic gloom.
If I climb this mountain again, I shall send ahead
People with brooms to sweep the clouds away.

They got back to Nanking early in the sixth month, having been away for almost two months. Happily the weather remained cool till the end. Even a fortnight later he writes, 'In the sixth month it has been cloudy and cold, as though it were the second month. This year's great failure has been the south wind'. But the poem ends with the warning that it would be a mistake to throw away one's fan: 'for it cannot be supposed that the God of Summer has quite wound up his business'.

The year ends with a poem of recollection:

After I ceased to be Prefect of Nanking
For years I never strolled about the town.
But one night after crossing by the Peach Leaf ferry
I strolled for a while along the moonlit streets.
Someone sitting in a tea-house, directly he saw me,
Rose to his feet, and gave a startled cry:
'I cannot believe it! Is it really Prefect Yuan?
Why, you are looking quite an old man!'
To hear this gave me an unpleasant feeling;
I did not feel old myself; but this man was startled.

I do not know what there was that day in my appearance
That made him take directly he saw me, this depressing view.
A long time has passed since then—over twenty years;
If the same man were to see me now he would indeed be startled!

In the middle of the second month, 1784, again accompanied by Liu Chih-p'eng, he set out for Chao-ch'ing, near Canton, to visit his brother Yuan Shu, who was now Governor there.

In his poem of final instructions he says:

At the time of the sacrifices send someone to the tombs at Hangchow;
When my married daughter comes on a visit sweep for her the new room.
If it rains much, see to it that book-worms don't ruin my books;
In the autumn be sure in good time to protect my orchids from the frost.
One thing only weighs on my mind: I shall not now be able
To put my two boys through their paces and see that they stick to their books.

He took with him a vast number of books, a light carrying-chair, especially designed for use on mountains, and a long list of the things his children wanted him to buy for them at Canton. 'Too lazy to open the calendar and choose a lucky day', he merely started when he happened to be ready to start. It was snowing hard, and he felt somewhat daunted at the thought of facing so long a journey at the age of sixty-eight, till he suddenly remembered that when he was a child he had been told how his great-grandfather, Yuan Hsiang-ch'un, had made a trip to Canton at the age of eighty. He went by boat up the Yangtze, visiting and duly writing poems about many spots with literary or historic associations. At Ch'ai-sang, near Kiukiang, he was shown 'the rock on which T'ao Ch'ien (died A.D. 427) lay when drunk':

It was not unusual for T'ao to get drunk,
And on one such occasion he slept on this rock,

With the strange result that a scrubby piece of stone
Has been cherished and admired for more than a thousand years.
Golden couches and jade stools have always existed in plenty;
But does anyone know the names of those who have taken a nap upon them?
They cannot compare with this rock that dominates Ch'ai-sang
More completely than an obelisk ten thousand cubits high.

Crossing lake P'o-yang he came to Nan-ch'ang where the dramatist Chiang Shih-ch'üan was then living. There had been rumours that he was dead, or was dying. It was not so bad as that; but Yuan Mei found that he had had a stroke and was paralysed on the right side, and his speech was affected. But he could still communicate by writing with his left hand, and his mind was as lively as ever. He and Yuan were both grateful to a contrary wind that delayed the departure of the travellers for several days; for it seemed unlikely that they would ever meet again.

They arrived at Chao-ch'ing in the middle of the fourth month. Yuan made many new friends among the officials of the place and was indefatigable in excursions to mountains, lakes and monasteries. But he was never quite happy in Kwangtung. He had heard much about the beauty of the singing-girls on the house-boats at Canton:

It is laughable that these River ladies have such a reputation;
On my first arrival they utterly damped my ardour for 'looking at flowers'.
When puffing flame from their blue lips they stood at the cabin-door;
I shrank away, for their clammy smell was like a ghost's hand.

It was annoying here too not to understand the local dialect, which is indeed so different from northern Chinese as to be almost a different language. He had been told that at Canton it was never hot in summer, which turned out, this year at any rate, to be far from true. On top of all this came devastating floods at Chao-ch'ing, at a time when Yuan Mei's brother was away at Canton. The Governor's residence stood on high ground, and was soon besieged by officials and townsmen, 'with all their belongings', whose homes had been inundated. Yuan Mei, who had been left in charge, was in favour of giving them shelter. He was afraid his brother's wife might object, but found that she was already determined 'to share, for good or ill, the fortunes of the city' that her husband ruled. 'Soon the officials were lodged in the main house, the townsfolk in out-houses, and smoke from improvised kitchens was rising in every part of the Governmental compound.' It was a fortnight before the floods subsided and the guests were able to go home.

At Canton he met Sun Shih-i (1720–1796), who had recently become Governor of Kwangtung province. Sun, after a rather chequered career, was soon to become one of the two or three most important statesmen of the late eighteenth century. He was himself something of a poet, and he was a friend both of Chiang Shih-ch'üan the dramatist and of Chao I, who along with Yuan Mei were considered the greatest writers of the time. In the next twelve years, while continually rising in eminence and often stationed in far-off places such as Tibet and Nepal, he remained Yuan Mei's staunch friend and supporter. Even in the midst of arduous duties at Lhasa, he found time 'by candle-light' to send a poem to Yuan Mei on the occasion of Yuan's eightieth birthday.

During an excursion to the Hsi-ch'iao Hills, about forty miles south-west of Canton, Yuan was taken ill with dysentery, and was obliged to hasten back to Chao-ch'ing. An extract of forsythia, which had done wonders on previous occasions, this time only made him worse. But he managed to make an excursion to the famous Lo-fu range, the refuge in old days of so many famous hermits and alchemists. Presumably Liu Chih-p'eng accompanied him on these trips, but we hear little about him, save for one curious episode: 'The door-keeper at Prefect Wu's house was a lad of sixteen called Yuan Shih-chin. He was very intelligent and a good singer. The moment he set eyes on Liu Chih-p'eng he took a great fancy to him and the two struck up a passionate friendship. It was very difficult for them to meet in private. After several vain attempts to do so they had at last managed to make a date, when the Prefect received an urgent summons to Canton. He had to rush off like a flash, and the boy was obliged to go with him. When he and Liu Chih-p'eng parted by the river-side their tears fell "like a well-rope".'

On the sixteenth day of the ninth month, the two travellers set out for home, intending to reach Nanking by the end of the year. They proceeded by boat to Kuei-lin where, nearly fifty years ago, Yuan Mei had visited his uncle and received from Governor Chin the precious recommendation to the Peking authorities that had launched him on his career. When they were nearing Kuei-lin, Yuan Mei fell ill again. But this time he made up his mind not to take any medicine, 'so as not to be like Wang Wei (A.D. 415–443) who took the excessive precaution of never stirring an inch unless he had a dose of calamus with him'.

In the poems written while he was at Chao-ch'ing we get very little impression of his relations with his brother and the rest of the household. But in a poem written when nearing Kuei-lin he tells us how he dreamt he was back in his brother's house, and for the first time we learn something of his life at the Hall of Evening Fragrance:

My brother's wife was cooking the farewell dinner.
I saw that her eyes were not better yet;
But she was gay and affectionate as ever.
Miss Wu soon served the dishes,
With a hand raised to hold her combs in place.
The girl Tun is talking so cleverly,
Intelligence lighting her whole face.
The boy Tuan is busy learning to walk;
Hopsy-daisy his little legs straddle.
This time he does not ask me to hold him;
He knows when I go he will have to shift for himself.

I in my dream was sad at this last dinner,
But happy for the moment still to be at home.

But the cock crowed; he woke, and the jagged mountains at the open window derided his dream. At this point he records one or two poems made during the journey by Liu Chih-p'eng. One is about their evening game of draughts:

After supper we generally play a few rounds of draughts;
Tonight I have privately decided to keep the shutters closed.
For why was it that yesterday I lost that first game?
Suddenly I saw through the cabin-window several curious peaks.

And again:

Once upon a time an old monkey and a double-blazoned peacock
Agreed to go a journey together, and rode in the same boat.
They screamed and hooted, seeming to show an interest in hills and streams.
Perhaps such creatures share with Man a love of scenery?

Liu called Yuan 'monkey' because in Chinese *yuan* means 'monkey'. Yuan Mei himself was fond of saying that in a previous incarnation he had been a white monkey on the hill beside his house. One must suppose that Yuan nicknamed Liu 'peacock' because of his preoccupation with his own appearance. Liu was diffident about his own poems and hesitated to publish them. But after his return to Nanking, Yuan Mei persuaded Liu to let him get some of them printed, on condition that there were not to be more than three hundred, the number that (according to legend) had satisfied Confucius when he edited the *Book of Songs*. The little volume was called *Liang-yueh Yu-ts'ao*, 'Travel sketches of Kwangtung and Kwangsi'. I do not know whether it still exists.

They intended on the way back to visit Kiukiang, which on their outward journey they had omitted to do. The place is always associated with the famous ninth-century poet Po

Chü-i, who was exiled there in A.D. 815 'People always say', remarks Yuan Mei, 'that in my poetry I imitate Po Chü-i. But I must confess with shame that till this year (1784) I had never done anything more than make a cursory examination of his works. But this time, before starting for home, I borrowed a copy of his *Ch'ang Ch'ing Chi* (Po Chü-i's collected works) and read it in the boat. I realized then that there were resemblances, though no more intentional on my part than was Yang Huo's personal likeness to his master Confucius. But there are two important differences between us. I am not a great drinker, and I do not "fawn upon" Buddha.'

At Kuei-lin he found a flourishing poetry club. He attended their meetings, and went excursions with them. When he left they hired a boat and accompanied him a long way towards the frontier of Kwangsi province. Before climbing (or rather, being carried up) the Heng Shan (about 4,300 feet), generally known as the Southern Peak, he stayed with the Prefect of the district and discovered that one of his servants wrote poetry. One used to be told that 'every Chinese coolie is a poet'. But this was evidently not Yuan Mei's opinion. He was astonished to find that this young servant wrote poetry; and a house-servant in China is of course far above a coolie in education and standing. 'He was a young man of about twenty', Yuan Mei writes. 'When he saw my visiting-card, he was delighted and rushed off to tell everyone at the Prefectual office that they were in luck's way —they were going to meet Yuan Mei, the poet. Presently the Prefect invited me to take a drink, and told this young man, whose name was Chang Pin, to show me some of his verses. I remember the couplet:

By the lake side the scented grasses join;
Beyond the mountain the goatsucker sings.

And again,

Over distant peaks a grey cloud keeps its high course;
Over the flat lake the firefly's torch halts, and skims again.

Indeed, a most unusual house-servant! Poetry was the only thing in life that he cared for. The Prefect once gave him some money to get married with. But instead of taking a wife, he spent it all on buying books.'

In the neighbourhood of Lake Tung-t'ing and along the Yangtze towards Hankow there were innumerable sites rich in poetic associations, but difficult to write about, because so many thousand of poets had preceded him. He had the luck, however, to reach the celebrated Yellow Crane Pagoda, near Wu-ch'ang, in the twelfth month, a time of year when poetic travellers generally stay at home. 'The Yellow Crane Pagoda under Snow' was therefore a comparatively unhackneyed theme, and to see snow except in his own garden was a sensation that he had not experienced for thirty years. But he was beginning to be tired of wandering, and in his poem wishes that the Yellow Crane after which the pagoda was named would take him on its back and carry him so swiftly to Nanking that he would be in time to see the first plum-blossom opening in his garden.

Arriving eventually at Kiukiang, Yuan Mei was moved rather by the association of the place with that great patron of poetry, T'ang Ying, than by memories of the ancient poet, Po Chü-i. T'ang Ying (*c.* 1680–1760) was Inspector of Customs at Kiukiang round about the middle of the eighteenth century. Yuan Mei numbers him among the great encouragers and lovers of poetry who flourished at that time, but who forty years later seemed to have no successors. All this enthusiasm 'suddenly became extinct'. 'When T'ang Ying was in charge of the Customs at Kiukiang, he hung up paper, ink, brushes and inkstone at the Lute Pavilion, and the Customs officials had orders to report the names of any travellers who inscribed poems there. He would then go and read the poems, sort out the good ones, and get into touch with their authors, to whom he presented answering poems. He set up a mausoleum in memory of Po Chü-i and put a statue of himself at the side of it. But when I passed through Kiukiang in the year *chia-ch'en* (1784) it had been turned into a theatre, and the statue of T'ang Ying had disappeared.' There was a certain appropriateness in the conversion of this building into a theatre; for T'ang Ying, in addition to his many other activities, was a prolific dramatist.

The name of T'ang Ying is very familiar to collectors of Chinese pottery, owing to the fact that he was director of the Imperial Porcelain Manufactory at Ching-te Chen (about 100 miles south-east of Kiukiang) at various periods in the first half of the eighteenth century. A good deal is said about him in most books on Chinese pottery; but it is only as a patron of poetry that he here concerns us.

A strong contrary wind held them up at P'eng-tse, about sixty miles down the Yangtze from Kiukiang, and it became obvious, since it was now the 26th of the twelfth month, that they would not get home till after the New Year. He grumbles at the snobbery of the wind, which so often obsequiously wafts along the bannered galleons of great officials or the deep-laden barges of rich merchants, but ignores the appeals of an aged traveller. The wind in reply points out the advantages of passing the New Year on board ship:

At home you would have to put on your best shoes
And bustle round paying New Year calls.
Your doors would be blocked with hundreds of red festoons;
Your ears deafened by the noise of bamboo-crackers.
How much better to be still on your journey,
Free to enjoy yourself in peace and quiet.
On New Year's day you need not wear hat and robe
When the boatmen wish you many happy returns. . . .
You can go on shore and find plum-blossom to look at;
You will make some extra poems for people to read.
In the first month the weather will be just right
To begin again singing songs of return.

He got home on the eleventh day of the first month, 1785. Last spring, during his absence, several high officials, attached to the retinue of the Emperor when he made his tour to the South, had looked for Yuan Mei and left behind poems and messages regretting his absence. But the most signal mark of honour paid to him was that the great Manchu official Ho-shen had sent someone to paint a picture of his garden. Ho-shen, a member of the Imperial Bodyguard, is said to have been first noticed by the Emperor Ch'ien Lung in 1775 when he was on guard at one of the palace gates. He at once became a favourite and was continually promoted. Ch'ien Lung, as he grew older, became less and less able to deal with public affairs, and eventually Ho-shen was virtual ruler of China, and remained so till Ch'ien Lung's death in 1799, when the new Emperor, Chia-ch'ing, forced Ho-shen to commit suicide. All that we know about him proceeds either from the flatterers that surrounded him during Ch'ien Lung's lifetime, or from the enemies who eventually compassed his ruin. This makes it difficult to estimate what sort of man he really was. As an administrator he was probably even more corrupt than was usual at the time; but he also seems to have been possessed of good abilities. The one point upon which all accounts agree is that he was very good-looking. Both Ho-shen and his brother Ho-lin were great admirers of Yuan Mei's writings, and he exchanged many poems with them in later days.

He wrote on his return:

The owner of this garden really thinks that his courage is something to boast of;
At sixty-eight he ran off to where the sky ends,
Covering a distance that cannot be less than 13,000 leagues.
He listened to the waves, listened to the winds and came laughing home.

And again:

When I reached the steps a fluttering snow of blossom struck my face;
What a joy, amid such fragrance, to take off one's travelling dress.

My old wife says with a smile, pointing at my concubines:
'If it had not been for the plum-blossom, you would never have come home!'

About Liu Chih-p'eng ('the peacock') he wrote:

The double-blazoned peacock, dressed up in his town clothes
Is turning the head of every boy and girl in Nanking.
Hoping that this will perhaps induce him to spread his emerald tail
The ladies on their promenades are wearing their heaviest rouge.

And finally:

Turning once more to the books I left, I am unendurably happy;
But this much I have to tell, that the world had better know:
Do not think of any corner of the earth as far away;
All you need do is to wave your whip, and sometime you will get there!

He was now no longer commenting and collating. His reading was done solely for pleasure:

When I was young I loved reading books,
And probed into each phrase with meticulous care.
Now that I am old I still love reading books,
But as a distraction, and to get the general meaning.
A moment later, I have forgotten what I read;
But whatever I have glanced at becomes part of me.
The flavour of a book lingers in my breast,
Tasting sweeter than a draught of old wine.

In the summer he wrote:

If at seventy I still plant trees,
Lookers-on, do not laugh at my folly.
It is true of course that no one lives forever;
But nothing is gained by knowing so in advance.

In 1785 the great text-collator Lu Wen-ch'ao (1717–1795), who had hitherto worked chiefly in the north, came to Nanking to direct the Chung-shan Academy. He was a useful friend because he constantly borrowed books and returned them with the text supplemented and corrected:

When other people borrow books, they borrow them and that is all;
But when you come to borrow a book my heart leaps for joy.
Every book you take away comes back in ten days
With every gap filled in, every mistake corrected.
You tell me that collating texts is the great passion of your life—
To sort them out with as fine precision as a sieve sifts rice;
That to get a single right meaning is better than a ship-load of pearls,
To resolve a single doubt is like the bottom falling off the bucket.

The Zen-master Ch'ing-liao (died *c.* A.D. 1152) was watching some meal being cooked in a bucket, when the bottom of the bucket fell out. The monks cried out, 'What a sad waste!' But Ch'ing-liao said, 'On the contrary, the shock was well worth the loss of a bucketful of meal'.

In the preface to his *Ch'ün Shu Shih Pu* ('Textual Notes on Various Books') Lu Wen-ch'ao mentions that Huang Teng-hsien (1709–1784) once said to him, 'Most people read books merely for their own advantage. But when *you* read, the book benefits as well'. Lu Wen-ch'ao knew that the remark was meant sarcastically and was a criticism of his frequent emendations. Yuan Mei's whole-hearted appreciation of his scribbled notes must have been a consolation to him.

In the autumn of 1786 Yuan Mei and his young friend Liu Chih-p'eng set out for the Wu-i Mountains, the great tea-growing centre. The Oxford Dictionary tells us that Bohea (the local pronunciation of Wu-i) is 'black tea of the lowest quality'. This is odd; for in China Wu-i tea is reckoned as one of the choicest kinds, and Yuan Mei evidently regarded it as having a tremendous reputation. It was drunk by the experts in minute cups, 'about as large as a bullet', which they constantly refilled. 'It was comical', he says, 'that these drinking men were like birds drinking.' He was told that the leaf must be plucked exactly at the right moment, dried according to a secret recipe, boiled in exactly the right way, and drunk with the proper formalities:

I had heard so much about this tea, that with great circumspection
I sipped at it, so as not to miss the 'flavour that is beyond flavour'.
In the little cup, after it was empty, a perfume still lingered;
I touched it gently with my tongue; the cup still tasted sweet. . . .

One night on the way to Wu-i he heard someone on a neighbouring boat telling wonder-tales. He invited him to come on board his own ship, and the story-teller, delighted to find a new audience, began to pour out ghost story after ghost story. Soon (as happens when ghosts are invoked) 'the lantern began to burn blue and a chilly blast shot in at the cabin window'. Some of these stories probably figure in the supplement to his earlier collection of ghost stories.

Liu Chih-p'eng had a passionate love of mountain scenery, and during this journey he continually rushed up to Yuan Mei's carrying-chair with new landscape poems:

Young Liu's inspiration, apparent on the whole journey,
Is doubly pure when our way lies through mountain scenery.
A successful verse makes him prouder than if he had taken a Degree;
He rushes up to the carrying-chair to show it to his old teacher.

On the return journey they stayed for a while in Hangchow and seem to have been back in Nanking by the end of the year (1786).

CHAPTER SEVEN

Poetry Talks and the Cookery Book

TO the summer of 1787 belongs the poem:

When one is old, one treasures every minute;
A single day is precious as a whole year.
And how seldom, even in a whole year,
Does a true rapture of the senses come one's way!
Man is born to get pleasure where he can;
How he sets about it depends on how he is made.
All that matters is to find out in good time,
Each for himself, which things he really enjoys.
I was born with many strong cravings;
Now that I am old they are gradually slipping away.
There are only left two or three things
That still delight me as they did in former days—
To spread out a book beside a bamboo-stream,
To run my fingers along an ancient jade,
To climb a hill with a stout stick in my hand,
To drink wine in the presence of lovely flowers,
Talk of books—why they please or fail to please—
Or of ghosts and marvels, no matter how far-fetched.
These are excesses in which, should he feel inclined,
A man of seventy-odd may well indulge.

And again:

I remember how when I was only eleven or twelve
I loved books more dearly than life itself.

Whenever I came to a stall where books were sold
I read and read, my feet rooted where I stood.
But alas I had no money to buy books;
I could only dream I had bought them, when I came home.
Yet of all the notes and extracts I still possess,
More than half were made in those early days.
When I got a post and had money to spend
I bought so many that they filled the whole house.
Now that I am old I still read them at night,
Not stopping till I have burnt a whole candle.
My two boys, at the age that I was then,
Look at a book without the least emotion.
It is not a thing to which one can ever be trained;
It all depends on one's karma *in former lives.*
A General's son does not become a General;
Great writers found no dynasties.
But it is *sad that a Yuan who is growing up,*
When faced with a book, merely heaves a sigh!

In a letter of 1788 Yuan Mei thanks Pi Yuan for agreeing to pay the cost of printing Yuan's *Poetry Talks* (Shih Hua) on which he had been working for many years. Since the 11th century hundreds of books with this title had been written. They tended to be anecdotal and informal in style, with a very wide range of contents, including stories about poets, discussions of technique, fragments of autobiography, reflexions on the true nature of poetry, and so on. In Yuan's book the typical form is an anecdote, leading up to a poem. For example: 'Wang Chi-tsu was my fellow-examiner in the year *chia-tzu* (1744). In the examination room he recited to himself a poem he had made, called "Passing by an ancient tomb". It ran:

Gloomy and forbidding the ancient tomb lowers;
A screech-owl stands on the sculptured arch.
Yet on the day when the mourners met at the interment
What a tumult of horses and carriages there was!

I told him I could not see why he was so pleased with it. Wang laughed and said: "Just shut your eyes and think".'

Yuan interpreted the title *Poetry Talks* in a very wide sense. Sometimes he gives anecdotes without poems, and sometimes (though he often insists that the book is not an anthology) poems without anecdotes. Some entries, especially in chapter 15, are purely learned, and seem as though they ought rather to have been included in his *Sui Pi*. There are a few scattered remarks about ancient poets; but in the main he deals with poets of the eighteenth century. There are a great many autobiographical references, and the book is one of our main sources of information about the details of his career. I shall translate here some of the passages in which he discusses poetry in general rather than particular poets or poems. In some cases, as will be seen, he is quoting remarks on poetry made by other people, but with which he was in agreement. Such extracts are, of course, no less interesting and relevant than the passages in which he directly expresses his own views.

But it will make the *Poetry Talks* easier to understand if, before giving these excerpts, I say something about the main controversies that divided critics of poetry in the eighteenth century. Put briefly, Yuan's own position was that literature has domains of its own and need not necessarily be a vehicle for moral edification, that it need not be written in close imitation of some approved ancient period or individual great master, and that it cannot become 'great' by borrowing phrases and even whole lines from the great writers of the past. Literature and especially poetry, Yuan Mei maintained, is above all an expression of individual temperament and feeling and, within the general framework of traditional technique, that temperament must find its own phrasing, its own idiom.

But the doctrine that literature has no value unless it is the 'vehicle' of moral instruction (*wen i tsai tao*) has always been part and parcel of orthodox Confucianism. The counter-claim that literature has rights of its own dates at least as early as the thirteenth century; but it has generally been the view of a small, sporadic opposition. This opposition had indeed some influence at the turn of the sixteenth and seventeenth centuries, and maintained a footing down to Yuan Mei's time. But the idea that literature has the right to an independent existence was not (any more than it is in China today) the normal view of writers, statesmen, or educators. Along with the orthodox creed that literature should be edifying, generally went a number of other views not logically connected with this main contention; for example the idea (similar to our notion of 'good' Latin, meaning Ciceronian Latin) that one must imitate the poetry of the T'ang dynasty (and preferably the eighth, not the ninth century) rather than that of the Sung dynasty; or again the idea that the more completely one's writing consists of tags from the great writers of the past, the 'greater' it will be. The principal exponent of the orthodox, didactic and archaistic school was Shen Te-ch'ien (1673–1769), of whom some account must here be given. In some ways he was extremely precocious: he wrote correct verse at the age of five and was teaching other children at the age of ten. But he was so bad at examinations that it was only at his eighteenth attempt that in 1739, at the age of 66, he managed to get his Third Degree. It was at this period, in Peking, that he and Yuan first met. For some reason the Emperor Ch'ien Lung took an immense fancy to him and at the age when most officials were thinking of retiring he suddenly found himself the recipient of innumerable Imperial favours and was entrusted with the editing of many official literary projects. On his own account he edited a number of anthologies, which have become famous. Here we are chiefly concerned with his Ming poetry anthology (1739), and his *Kuo Ch'ao Pieh Ts'ai Chi* (1759), an anthology of Manchu dynasty poems. The latter only included poems by writers who were no longer alive, so that there was no question of Yuan Mei himself figuring in it. But, partly perhaps as a friendly gesture towards him, some poems by his unfortunate sister Su-wen (Yuan Chi) were included.

Shen Te-ch'ien, who was living at Soochow, went to Peking in 1761 to take part in the celebrations that were to mark the entry of the Emperor's mother into her seventieth year. He brought the new anthology with him and asked the Emperor to write a preface. Ch'ien Lung refused to do so for four reasons. I will enumerate them here, for they show what pitfalls lay in the path of an eighteenth-century Chinese anthologist:

(1) He had included poems by the Ming dynasty official and poet Ch'ien Ch'ien-i (1582–1664) who had submitted to the Manchus in 1645, but had afterwards (so it was said) attacked them in his writings. The Emperor subscribed to the didactic theory of poetry in its most extreme form. 'What is poetry?', he said, in reference to the inclusion of Ch'ien Ch'ien-i's poems in the anthology. 'It is an expression of the writer's loyalty to the Throne and piety towards his parents. Poetry that does not fulfil these functions, I do not count as poetry at all. . . . Such too is the doctrine to which Shen Te-ch'ien has himself always subscribed; but the present anthology is at complete variance with his principles.'

(2) He had included poems by a certain Ch'ien Ming-shih, who (*c.* 1730) had been branded as a 'traitor to Confucianism'. (The truth, however, seems to be that Ch'ien Ming-shih had merely been victimized because he knew too much about the questionable methods by which Ch'ien Lung's father had got himself installed as Emperor.)

(3) He had referred in the anthology to an uncle of the Emperor by his personal name instead of by his title, 'a liberty that even I, the Emperor, would not have taken'.

(4) That though the names in the anthology were supposed to be in chronological order, numerous mistakes of date had been made.

The anthology was handed over to members of the Hanlin Academy to be thoroughly overhauled and was finally published in its present form, with a preface by the Emperor.

At a time when this anthology was already in existence,

but probably before it had incurred the Emperor's displeasure, Yuan Mei addressed two letters to its compiler. It is clear that when he wrote the second letter he had only heard about the contents of the anthology (probably from one of Shen's numerous assistants), but had not actually seen it. This must also be true of the earlier letter. The first letter, which only refers incidentally to the anthology, is chiefly an attack on Shen Te-ch'ien's theory that only T'ang poetry and not Sung poetry should be studied. Yuan goes on to ask why Shen Te-ch'ien had included in his anthology so large a number of poems by Li E (1692–1752), the great advocate of Sung poetry, and so few by Ch'ien Ch'ien-i, the opponent of archaistic imitation. To this Shen Te-ch'ien might well have answered that in giving space to a poet whose work he did not like and whose theories he disapproved of, he was showing the impartiality of a good anthologist. And he might have added that as Ch'ien Ch'ien-i was not *persona grata* with the ruling dynasty, he thought it imprudent to give him too much space. As we have seen, it proved in the outcome to have been a grave indiscretion to include Ch'ien Ch'ien-i at all. The second letter begins: 'I hear that in your anthology you have left out Wang Yen-hung (*c.* 1620–1680) on the ground that he wrote love-poetry, from which no moral instruction can be derived.' He then goes on to point out (as he does in many other places) that Confucius did not exclude love-poems from the *Book of Songs*. An anthologist, Yuan says, is a sort of historian, and must record every kind of poetry that was produced in the age with which he is dealing; otherwise he is a false historian. Love-poetry and poetry about Court ladies are recognized categories of literature and no historian of literature has any business to exclude them. Love-poetry (*yen-tz'u*) was of course written in elaborate floral and other metaphors, and was never improper except by implication. But it was hardly ever included in a poet's collected works and even more seldom in an anthology. Yuan Mei's complaint was therefore rather unreasonable. To us *yen-tz'u* seem frigid, artificial and pedantic. The most famous example of such a poem which did find its way into an author's collected works during the Manchu dynasty was one in 400 lines written by the highly respected scholar Chu I-tsun (1629–1709) in 1669. It was composed in memory of his wife's sister, with whom it is evident that Chu was very much in love. The poem is a moraine of historical allusions, metaphors and euphuisms, some of them so obscure that the author felt obliged to explain them in notes. Yet so authorized and familiar was this way of handling love-themes that a modern writer, Mr. Fang Chao-ying, describes the poem as 'a straight-forward revelation of passion'. I find this description very interesting. It sets me wondering, for example, whether Ovid's countrymen may not have regarded his fluent artificialities in the same light. Chu I-tsun's poem is referred to more than once by Yuan Mei when he is arguing that love-poetry ought not to be excluded from collected works.

In a postscript he goes on to complain that Shen Te-ch'ien in his anthology of Ming poetry has singled out for praise a couplet by the seventeenth-century writer Liu Yung-hsi, even going so far as to say that these few words were 'worth more than a hundred poems by other men'. It consists, however (as Yuan Mei points out), entirely of tags from the ancients. The only exception, Yuan says, is the phrase 'In Heaven and Earth, thorns and brambles', which was a proverbial phrase meaning 'trouble everywhere', such as 'any village boy three feet high might have used'.

The tone of these letters is very off-hand. Shen was forty-three years older than Yuan, and in a country where respect has always been paid to the aged it comes as rather a surprise to find Yuan writing to him in the same bantering style that he used when addressing equals and contemporaries. But it must be remembered that they sat for the Third Degree together and were therefore in the scholastic sense contemporaries (*t'ung-nien*, 'same year'). Yuan Mei expressly states, in his *Poetry Talks*, that Shen Te-ch'ien did not answer the second letter, and we have no reason to suppose that he answered the first. But they remained on good terms and when Yuan was ill at Soochow in 1763 Shen Te-ch'ien called and, at the age of ninety, chattered tirelessly. A year later Shen visited Peking and on his way there or back was painted, along with Yuan and three other friends in a famous group ('Classic gathering in the Sui-yuan') by the portraitist Wu Hsing-ts'eng.

Here are a few of the passages in the *Poetry Talks* that deal with poetry in general.

> Someone asked me to name the best poetry that has been written during this dynasty. I replied by asking him which is the best poem in the *Book of Songs*. He could not answer. Poetry, I then told him, is like the flowers of the fields; in spring the orchid, in autumn the chrysanthemum. One cannot say that one is better than the other. Any poem that by its music and beauty of conception can move the heart is a good poem.
>
> Li Ch'ung-hua says: 'It is most important for poets to do a lot of reading. But this is only as a refreshment of the spirit. If neither the poet himself nor the reader knows exactly how this book-learning has affected a poem, then it is a true poem. But if he tries deliberately to dazzle us by the range of his reading, then at once he falls into an inferior category.'

(Li Ch'ung-hua was a critic of the traditionalist school, who took his Third Degree in 1724. Yuan Mei got to know him at Peking in early days and was a member of his Poetry Club.)

> Yang Wan-li said: 'Why is it that people with a low degree of natural capacity always talk such a lot about metre and tone-pattern, but disregard beauty of conception? Metre and tone-pattern are after all only the scaffolding, and it is easy enough to imitate them. But it is in

the conception of the poem that the poet's genius is expressed, and it is only here that his natural gifts come into play.'

[Yang Wan-li (A.D. 1124–1206), was a famous poet and critic. Yuan Mei more than once attributes this passage to him; but it does not, I think, occur in his surviving works.]

P'u Hsien said: 'Poetry is born in the heart and made by the hand. If it is the heart that controls the hand, then all is well; but if the hand does the heart's work, all is lost. Today those who make imitation the basis of poetry help themselves by taking a bit here and a bit there, all of it raked out of piles of old paper, instead of relying on what flows from their own feelings. That is what I call "the hand doing the heart's work"'.

(P'u Hsien was head of an Academy at Kuei-lin, and it was there that Yuan Mei met him in 1784.)

Wu Ying-fang said, 'In poetry the idea should be master and the words merely slaves of the idea. If the idea is too small and the words are too many, then it is like a weak man who has no control over his slaves; he calls, but they do not come'.

[Wu Ying-fang (A.D. 1702–1781), was spoken to rudely by an attendant when he went in for the Boys' Examination and felt so humiliated that he never went in for an examination again, and so never held office. But he had ample private means and was able to devote himself to music, poetry and archaeology.]

Tai Yü-jang has the line

The night air presses upon the hills, making them a foot lower.

The beauty of such a line is that it lies on the margin between the intelligible and the unintelligible.

(It is, in the original at any rate, indeed a wonderful line; Tai was a younger Contemporary of Yüan Mei.)

I love all the old poets and I really cannot say that there is one that I like better than the rest. The same is true of modern poets. But I have a special liking for the poetry of Kao Ch'i-cho and Huang Jen. I suppose I am near them in temperament.

[Kao Ch'i-cho (A.D. 1676–1738) and Huang Jen (A.D. 1683 – *c.* 1764) were poets famous at the beginning of the eighteenth century, but to a large extent forgotten afterwards. Probably Yuan Mei's affection for their works was partly due to his having read them as a boy, when they first came out].

The division of poetry into 'T'ang style' and 'Sung style' is still rigidly maintained. This is to ignore the fact that poetry is the product of human feeling, whereas T'ang and Sung are the names of dynasties. Feelings do not change with each fresh dynasty.

Yuan Mei, it is obvious from his correspondence with Shen Te-ch'ien and others, as also from the above extracts from the *Poetry Talks*, shared some of the views of the early nineteenth century European romantics. If he could have read in Stendhal's *Racine et Shakespeare*: 'Romanticism is the art of furnishing the public with a literature which, given the current state of its habits and feelings, is calculated to produce the maximum amount of pleasure. Classicism, on the contrary, aims at reproducing the sort of literature which gave the greatest possible pleasure to our great-grandfathers', Yuan would certainly have recognized himself as at any rate a quasi-romantic. But a break with the forms of the past was only one side of romanticism. Manzoni, looked upon as the father of the movement, believed it to be the duty of the poet to 'foster in the soul [of his reader] the ideals of justice and humanity'. Manzoni, then, though he both called himself and was accepted as a romantic, believed that literature has an ethical mission, and reading such passages Yuan Mei would have seen at once that the alignment in Europe was quite different from that in China, where almost all the didacticists were also upholders of traditional rules and restrictions, and it would have surprised him to find Manzoni the moralist denouncing the Aristotelian Unities, and such rules as that the action in a tragedy must necessarily take place within the precincts of a king's palace! Nor would he have been quite at home with Stendhal's view that the poet writes in order to give the greatest possible pleasure to other people. Anxious though Yuan was to be successful and widely esteemed as an author, he always represents the function of the poet as being to express his own temperament, his own pleasures and preferences rather than to give 'le plus grand plaisir possible' to others. Still less was the state of hectic emotional disturbance that we associate with rather later and particularly with German romanticism one that Yuan Mei demanded from the poet or indeed had himself ever experienced.

In 1788 Yuan Mei's protector Sun Shih-i, whom he had met four years before in Canton, was sent to Annam to quell a rebellion against the reigning dynasty. He was at first very successful, and in 1789 Yuan Mei addressed to him a long poem congratulating him on his victory. But this turned out to be premature. Fresh rebel forces appeared on the scene, the Chinese were defeated, and after spending untold quantities of life and treasure in a vain effort to uphold the reigning dynasty, the Chinese government suddenly decided that it made no difference whatever to China who reigned over Annam, and the Nguyen dynasty, supplanting the Li dynasty, was tamely recognized, and ruled over Annam till recent times. Sun Shih-i got off lightly and in 1790 was made Governor-General of Kiangnan and Kiangsi, with his headquarters at Nanking. Once more Yuan Mei had a great friend and supporter close at hand.

When Yuan was at Chao-ch'ing near Canton, staying with his brother in 1784, he made the acquaintance of a frail bookish person called P'eng Chu, who asked to be enrolled as his pupil. P'eng Chu was at the time Prefect of Hsiang-shan, the island on which lies the Portuguese colony of Macao. In the autumn of 1789 there suddenly appeared at Yuan Mei's door a man with a peacock feather in his hat and very smart clothes. It turned out to be P'eng Chu, who was on his way to Peking to receive a decoration from the Emperor. The story he told was a surprising one. In 1789 the Kwangtung coast was ravaged by a pirate-king named the Wave-leveller. The authorities at Hsiang-shan got into trouble for failing to deal with him. At this point P'eng Chu startled them by offering to resign his Prefectship and deal with the pirate himself. Accompanied by two hundred marines he performed prodigies of organization and valour in routing the pirate flotilla, and captured seven hundred of them alive. He stayed with Yuan Mei for three days, and when at his departure Yuan offered him some help, to get him comfortably to Peking, 'he refused everything, but only asked for Mr. Hsu of K'un-shan's *Explanation of the Nine Classics*, some books of anecdotes, and collected works by T'ang and Sung authors. Then, his boat deeply laden with books, he went off to Peking'. He died, aged 59, in 1792.

Having failed in an attempt to get his Second Degree, Liu Chih-p'eng was threatening to go to Peking and see what he could pick up in the way of a job. The news perturbed Yuan Mei:

Since I heard this news about your thinking of going to Peking
I have been so wretched that I have not slept for several nights on end.
It is true that the beauty of the journey alone would make it worth your while;
But is it so easy for master and pupil to part after ten years . . . .?

However, only a few months later a Manchu official called Fu, who had been appointed Intendant of the Kiukiang region, about 200 miles up the Yangtze, passed through Nanking and called on Yuan Mei. He took a fancy to a Buddhist picture belonging to Yuan, called 'An Angel scattering Flowers', which Yuan reluctantly presented to him. He also apparently took a fancy to Liu Chih-p'eng and offered to take him to Kiukiang as his secretary. Kiukiang was, of course, not nearly so far off as Peking, and this time Yuan Mei seems to have resigned himself to losing Liu, at any rate for the time being. He started on the eighteenth day of the tenth month, the exact ten years anniversary of the date on which they had first met. 'This', Yuan wrote, 'wears the aspect of an arrangement planned by Heaven from the start, and I must not grieve at our parting.' In his poem to Liu's employer he said laughingly:

At Kiukiang by this time the winter winds are blowing;
It is well that you have a secretary and a picture to amuse you on the way.
But at one blow to be deprived of a pupil and an angel—
This surely is a grave abuse of high official power!

Shortly before Liu Chih-p'eng went to Kiukiang his wife died at the age of about twenty-four. She was buried on ground given to him by Yuan, who also made the spring-time offerings at her grave on Liu's behalf, while he was at Kiukiang.

A soothsayer had once prophesied that Yuan Mei would have a son at the age of 62 and would die at the age of 75. At the end of 1790 he again had a long bout of stomach-trouble and it seemed as though the soothsayer, whose prophecy about Yuan's son had come true, would prove right again about the year of his death. He took the precaution of writing a dirge on his own death, and he invited his friends to write on the same theme, using any form or rhyme that they liked. The dirge ends:

Who knows but I shall wander to some Heaven beyond the Heavens,
Where my eyes shall see things they have never seen?
It would be too dull if the Wheel of transmigration
Merely fashions a poet, as it did before.

The response to his invitation was very poor. Most of his friends felt that to write about a living man as though he were dead was 'unlucky'—that in fact the theme was too macabre. He was obliged to send a whip-up, in which he explained that they were taking the whole matter too solemnly. He had hoped they would just read his dirge, smile, and 'help themselves to another cup of wine'. Among those who responded to the invitation to write poems 'in answer' to his self-dirge was the celebrated scholar and educationalist Yao Nai (1731–1815). They had met casually a few years before, but it was not till 1790, when Yao came to teach in the Chung-shan Academy at Nanking, that they became intimate. During the last eight years of Yuan Mei's life they were constantly together, and it was Yao who wrote Yuan Mei's tomb inscription. Yao was the great popularizer of a rather old-fashioned school of Confucianism which, largely owing to his textbooks, dominated the Chinese educational outlook till recent times. He was a man of deeply serious and earnest character; but he did not allow Yuan Mei's ribald attacks on the Neo-Confucians or his disregard for Confucian proprieties to blind him to Yuan's merits as a writer or to the solid worth of his character. In his answering poem, hitting very dexterously the light tone that in Yuan's view the occasion demanded, he begs him at least to remain at his post till a suitable successor can be found.

Yao Nai stood very much upon his dignity and the contrast in this respect between him and Yuan Mei was once well summed-up by Liu Chih-p'eng. A young poet and painter called Kuo Lin (1767–1831) sent a painting to Yuan Mei, asking him to write an inscription on it. 'Knowing that I am old and feeble,' says Yuan, 'he was considerate enough to send a couple of verses along with the painting, and merely wanted me to copy them. I was delighted to do so, and in replying I thanked him for saving me trouble, and said that if the composing of the inscription had been left to me, I could not have done it nearly as well. Encouraged by this, he did the same to Yao Nai. But Yao thought it very bad manners and wrote round to several people complaining of the young man's rudeness. . . . My young friend Liu said: "You were both right. If there were no Yao Nai we younger people might easily forget what respect is due to elders, and if there were no Yuan Mei we should not know how large of mind an elder can be".' Kuo Lin was a rather bizarre young man, conspicuous by the fact that one of his eyebrows was snowy white.

In 1790 Yuan Mei's great admirer Sun Shih-i (shortly after his misadventures in Annam) became, as we have seen, Governor-General of the Nanking region, and at the same time it so happened that all the main officials at Nanking were writers of poetry. 'Never at any time was Nanking so cultivated', writes Yuan Mei in his *Poetry Talks*. So far from feeling (as in old age so many writers do) that he had outlived his public, he was at this period more in request both as a poet and a teacher of the art of poetry than at any previous time. At this time too his practice (so much criticized) of accepting lady pupils was at its height. It was maintained by his opponents both that this was an infringement of the Confucian precept that the sexes should not mingle, and that for women to receive a literary education at all (even at the hands of their mothers and sisters) was unnecessary and undesirable. Yuan Mei met the latter point (not very convincingly) by pointing out that the speakers in many of the poems in the *Book of Songs* were obviously women. However, his posthumous reputation scored by the attitude he took up on this question, and he was hailed in the nineteen-twenties as a pioneer defender of the rights of women. He had at this period thirteen principal lady-pupils, of whom a picture was once made. But in an anthology of 'Poems by my Lady Pupils' he includes work by no less than twenty-eight ladies. I will not burden you with a long list of names; but I think we may take as typical Chin I, called Hsien-hsien ('slender'). Frail, ailing, plaintive, doomed to an early death, she reminds one at once of Tai-yü, the heroine of the novel *Hung Lou Meng* (Dream of the Red Chamber), which was first printed in 1792. This resemblance had already occurred to me before I came across her poem 'On a cold night, waiting in vain for my husband to come home and reading the *Hung Lou Meng*', in which she says that the story exactly fits her case. She had a passionate admiration for Yuan Mei's poetry. He tells us that when she lay dying (1794) she was worried because there were passages in books she had been reading, about which she had meant to consult Yuan Mei. In a poem about her written shortly before his own death, Yuan says:

I am old, and we shall not be parted for very long;
Be sure to take good care of yourself in Heaven,
And let me find you with all your questions ready,
A smile on your face, waiting for me in the World Below.

In 1790 the Emperor Ch'ien Lung entered upon his eightieth year, and envoys from many foreign countries came to Peking to take part in the celebrations. Among them was the Korean official and poet P'o Ch'i-chia. Yuan Mei was told that this foreigner had offered high prices for Yuan's own works and for the little volume of Liu Chih-p'eng's poems, but 'could not get them and had gone away very much disappointed'. In the case of Liu's poems, which had been printed at Nanking probably in a very small edition, it was natural (since Liu had no sort of reputation as a poet) that the Peking bookshops could not supply them. Yuan's works, on the other hand, were certainly not unobtainable because there was no demand for them. They were, on the contrary, precisely at this time, having an immense vogue at Court, and were admired by several members of the Emperor's family, including Prince Li (Yung-en, 1727–1805), to whose own poems Yuan Mei wrote a preface. It is more likely then that the Korean failed to obtain Yuan's works because, owing to the heavy demand for them, the booksellers were out of stock. Both Yuan and his friends constantly allude to this enquiry for his works by a foreign envoy as proof of his immense fame at this period.

In a poem addressed to Liu Chih-p'eng at Kiukiang early in 1791, Yuan Mei recalled the scene of their parting:

Do you remember the scene of our parting, by the light of a solitary candle,
How we lay propped on the same pillow, listening for the cock to crow?
Suddenly I found to my own surprise that I was bitterly weeping.
The tears fell on your coat; are they dry or not?

To a series of reflective and reminiscent poems belongs the following:

Now that I am old, unable to endure seeing myself in the mirror,
I have thought of a way to escape the sight of my own decrepitude.
Kinder to me, when I dress my hair, is the shadow from my lamp;
It shows me on the wall, yet does not show the frost that lies on my brow.

Early in 1792 he started off on his second expedition to the T'ien-t'ai mountains. This time his companions were Chang P'ei, a gay young man of about twenty, rather on the pattern of Liu Chih-p'eng, and a certain Ho Lan-t'ing, who had been suggested to him as a son-in-law. 'If only I had more daughters', says Yuan, 'you should certainly have one of them.'

Naturally he thought often of Liu Chih-p'eng, with whom he had made the same expedition ten years before, and he writes to him that 'the peach-blossom this year looks slightly cross, as though reproaching me for not having brought Mr. Liu'. All did not go smoothly. A monk told him of a short cut. The path soon fizzled out and they found themselves fighting their way through precipitous jungle. Spokes fell out of the rickshaw wheels, the carriers were utterly worn out. 'I send this word to all men under Heaven,' writes Yuan Mei, 'never be in too much of a hurry. On the usual path everything is smooth and easy; short cuts get one all tied up. And those who give directions ought to remember that once one goes wrong there is often no turning back.' On the way to the Nan-ming Monastery he saw some cherries 'all red and fresh', but too high up to pick; so (at the age of seventy-six) he swarmed up the tree and ate them where they grew. He was indeed very much alive; but oddly enough just at this time a rumour got about that he was dead, and at Soochow a number of his friends met and performed the rites of formal lamentation. They were perhaps unable to believe that the soothsayer's prophecy had not come true.

When Yuan Mei was passing through Shao-hsing on his way back from the T'ien-t'ai, an acquaintance gave him an order for three copies of his Complete Works, paying at the rate of five ounces of silver (£1 13s. 4d.) per copy, in advance. 'When I got back to Nanking I sent him the three copies. Presently I got a letter saying that the invoice specified two copies, not three; but that there were traces of the figure having been tampered with. Only two copies arrived, and it seemed clear that the third had been stolen by the person to whom the commission had been entrusted.' The story gratified Yuan Mei, who assumed that the thief had a passionate desire to possess his works. He goes on to tell another story of an appreciative thief: 'The house of a certain rich man called Wu, at Hsien-chien (in Kiangsi) was invaded one night by seven thieves, carrying torches and cudgels. They fell upon Mr. Wu and trussed him up, handling him very roughly. When this had been done, they were joined by a handsome young man, very well dressed, who went up to the bookshelves and began inspecting the contents. He found a Sung edition of the *Wen Hsuan* anthology and a copy of my collected poems. He laughed, saying: "There are not many rich men who have the good taste to read Yuan Mei's works. Set Mr. Wu free!" So saying, he put the two books under his arm, and they all departed.' He goes on to tell how three other Koreans (in addition to P'o Ch'i-chia, already mentioned), Li Ch'eng-hsun, Li Chia-ming and Hung Ta-jung had all purchased his works at Peking and made enquiries about his way of life, age and so on.

Some light on his new young friend Chang P'ei who accompanied him on the second expedition to T'ien-t'ai, is thrown by the following story: 'One member of the ladies' poetry club at Hsi-leng (Hangchow) was a pupil of mine who was one of the handsomest women of the time. Chang P'ei determined at all costs to see her, so when I went to the meeting of the club, he disguised himself as a footman and walked behind my carrying-chair. It turned out, however, that the lady was unwell and had stayed at home, so he came back disappointed. Later in the day she sent me a note, asking me to come to her house and have a chat about poetry. Chang P'ei was delighted and, again disguised as a servant, he walked behind my chair. But when after walking for about two miles through heavy rain we reached the lady's house, there was someone there with whom he was acquainted, and frightened of being recognized, he turned and fled. He was already soaked to the skin, and on the way home he stumbled and fell into a ditch.'

It was, however, only for a short time that Chang P'ei played Liu Chih-p'eng's role as Yuan Mei's principal young companion; for in the ninth month of 1792 we find Liu back again at Nanking, playing the part of semi-host at Yuan Mei's house.

In the early part of 1793 Yuan stayed at Chenkiang, about fifty miles down the Yangtze from Nanking, with his lady-pupil

Lo Ch'i-lan, a young widow whom he considered very gifted. In the autumn, when he was back at Nanking, he was at last visited by Wu Sung-liang (1766–1834), a young Kiangsi man with an immense reputation both as a painter and a poet. At the age of about twenty he went to Peking and attracted the attention of many prominent writers. A few years later he already had an entourage of disciples. Yuan Mei first saw a poem by him in 1792 and was immensely struck by it. Next year in the spring a letter came from Yuan's friend Wang Yu-liang (1742–1797) in Peking, saying that he had given the poet Wu Sung-liang a letter of introduction to Yuan Mei; the young poet was on his way to the south and would soon be calling on Yuan in Nanking. 'I was enchanted', writes Yuan, 'and "swept a couch" to receive him. But six months passed before he came. However, when he at last arrived from Yangchow it was clear that he was indeed something quite out of the ordinary . . . ' Here the entry, which is from the unfinished supplement to the *Poetry Talks*, breaks off. Wu Sung-liang too wrote a book of *Poetry Talks* and in it he says that one of Yuan Mei's disciples hinted that he (Wu) ought not to let Yuan Mei treat him as an equal, but should behave towards Yuan as a pupil approaching a great master. Wu in an improvised stanza protested that so great a man as Yuan Mei must be utterly indifferent to the number of 'peach-trees and plum-trees' (i.e. disciples) who waited outside his gate. 'But so far from being unwilling to treat him as master, I felt embarrassed at being received as an equal.' It is evident that Yuan Mei admired Wu Sung-liang immensely and regarded him as a great friend. But Wu was not very attentive to his aged admirer; for in 1797 Yuan sent him a poem complaining that Wu had not written to him for over a year.

Few people today have heard of Wu Sung-liang; but the same is not true of another young poet with whom Yuan Mei got into touch a year later, in 1794. When the well-known writer Hung Liang-chi (1746–1809) was passing through Nanking, Yuan asked him about the young poets at Peking, and Hung at once named a Szechwan man called Chang

Wen-t'ao (1764–1814). 'I remembered', Yuan says, 'that when I went to the Capital for the Special Examination (1736) at Chao Ta-ch'ing's place I met a handsome young man called Chang Ku-chien. We got on together famously, and somehow I felt that this young poet Chang Wen-t'ao might be in some way related to him. I wrote to the young man and asked if this was so. He replied that Chang Ku-chien was his father. He told me that Ku-chien had reached the rank of Governor, and had then retired, but was still in robust health. This news, coupled with the fact that my old friend had so remarkable a son, delighted me extremely.' The father was living at his ancestral home at Sui-ning in Szechwan. 'How it would delight him', wrote the son, 'if you were to visit him there and let him take you up Mount O-mi.' Yuan, however, did not feel equal to the long journey to Szechwan. Unlike Wu Sung-liang, Chang Wen-t'ao is by no means forgotten. In 1798 he wrote a series of poems describing the sufferings of the common people during the suppression of the White Lotus Sect rebels. The revolt (which lasted for nine years) had like most such movements in China a religious, Taoist, colouring, but was in effect an uprising against the corrupt and oppressive rule of the Manchu regime. These poems have always been popular, and they now fit in very well with current directives as to what poetry should be.

In the summer of 1793 England's first Ambassador to China sailed up the coast of Chekiang in H.M.S. *Tiger*. It was at first naturally thought that the intruders were pirates, and there was great alarm. But it soon became apparent that they were merely barbarian envoys on their way to Peking, and interest in them subsided. The Ambassador and his suite returned in the autumn not by sea, but down the Grand Canal. Their return aroused far greater general curiosity than their arrival, and the banks of the Canal were thronged for miles on end by many thousands of spectators. Yuan Mei never mentions the mission, despite the fact that he not only knew of its existence, but also knew that it had acquired a copy of his complete works. This fact he must certainly have known, because it is referred to in a poem addressed to him by a friend on his eightieth birthday. 'Your reputation as a writer makes a stir beyond the seas', says T'ao Huan-yueh, adding the note, 'Korea, Ying-chi-li [England] and other countries bought Yuan Mei's Complete Works for a heavy price'. Another friend, Yo Shu-jen, also says, 'At the Capital a barbarian envoy asked about your recent movements', adding the note, 'This was the Ying-chi-li Country Envoy'.

There is obviously room for endless speculation as to which member of the English party bought Yuan Mei's works (for the expression 'envoy' need not necessarily mean Lord Macartney himself), who advised him to make the purchase, what has become of the book, and so on. The only point that interests us here is Yuan Mei's apparent indifference to an occurrence which evidently struck his friends as a notable testimony to the universality of his fame.

Early in 1794 Yuan Mei received four letters from members of the High Command operating against the Gurkhas of Nepal, who had been making raids into Tibet. One was from his friend and patron Sun Shih-i, who was acting as Quartermaster-General to the expedition. Even more gratifying were the other three letters, all from top-ranking Manchu grandees, none of whom he had ever met. The first was Fu-k'ang-an, who wrote: 'Since my childhood your name has been familiar to me as one of the great writers of our time; but I was in the north and you in the south, and I was never able to call upon you. . . . In the spring of *chia-ch'en* (1784) when I was in attendance upon the Emperor during his visit to Nanking, I had planned to come and see you, but was sent elsewhere by His Majesty, and was unable to do so. . . . Recently I have seen your *Poetry Talks* and *Ghost Stories*. These are, of course, light works, but they are infinitely superior to the *Poetry Talks* of Yen Yü (*c.* 1200) or the *New Tales of Yü Ch'u* (collected by Chang Ch'ao in 1683). I had those books of yours in my luggage, and constantly read them during the journey. Here in Tibet I have, during intervals in the fighting, seen a lot of Grand Secretary Sun Shih-i and of Governor-

General Hui-ling (1743–1804) and both of them spoke of you. His Excellency Ho-lin had with him a copy of your Complete Works, which I read, and was impressed by the vast range of your talents. . . . My present expedition has carried me far beyond Tibet, into country that has never previously been in communication with China, under circumstances so extraordinary that no genius less than yours could possibly describe them.

'When I was young I served in the Palace, but had no opportunity of reading the books in the Imperial Library. Later, I travelled to almost every part of the Empire, and saw many famous mountains and great rivers, but unfortunately lacked the power to celebrate them in song. I was therefore all the more impressed when I read your poems on such subjects.'

Hui-ling and Ho-lin wrote similar letters, which arrived by the same messenger. Shortly afterwards he received a letter from the Emperor's cousin, Hung-wu (d. 1811), to whom he had sent a copy of the *Poetry Talks*, saying that he had been longing to meet Yuan for thirty or forty years. These relations of the Emperor led a curious existence, locked away in the Forbidden City and intent upon proving, by a parade of unworldliness and exaggerated æstheticism, that they had no political aspirations. Hung-wu has something of a reputation as a painter.

In the summer the Governor of Chekiang province, Chang Chao-ching, sent Yuan Mei a European glass mirror so huge that it was difficult to get it through his front door. 'I have a passion for mirrors', he writes, 'and possess about thirty of them, some made of metal, some of glass. . . . But since this huge foreign mirror arrived, it has been as when the full moon mounts into the sky and all the stars fade out—my other mirrors no longer count at all.' Mirrors are supposed by their magic power to show what is going on in their owner's heart, and in his poem of thanks Yuan says that this huge mirror clearly shows the word 'gratitude' stamped upon 'this aged man's heart'. Long afterwards his grandson Yuan Tsu-chih wrote: 'Lady visitors were particularly frequent in spring and autumn. As they came through the garden, the flowers in their hair brushing the willow branches, they gave fresh beauty to the scene. There were mirrors everywhere at the Sui-yuan, as my grandfather had a great love of them. The ladies would take the opportunity of scanning themselves in the mirrors and putting their make-up to rights. If they got as far as my grandfather's own rooms, where the giant mirror was kept, they never failed to study themselves in it with the utmost assiduity, adjusting their sleeves and hitching up their drawers; and they would even go into the inner room and seat themselves there, leaving behind them a trail of scent that lasted for several days.' The great mirror, the grandson tells us, was seven foot square.

Late in the year Yuan Mei wrote a poem called 'My brush does not grow old':

Writing poems is like the blossoming of flowers;
If there is too much blossom the flowers are generally small;
And all the more, with a man nearing eighty,
Whose powers of invention have long withered away.
Yet all the same, people wanting poems
Continue to clamour for them all day long.
They know that the silkworm, till the moment of its death,
Never ceases to put out fresh threads.
I do my best to turn out something for them,
Though secretly ashamed to show such poor stuff.
Yet oddly enough my good friends that come
All accord in praising what I produce.
I am not the least shaken in my own belief;
But all the same I keep a copy in my drawer.
Can it be that though my body sinks to decay
My writing brush alone is still young?

On the second day of the third month, 1795, he celebrated his eightieth (or, as we in the West should say, seventy-ninth) birthday. He received over three thousand poems and letters of congratulation. From these he chose about two hundred and printed them in a separate little volume. Manchu princes and grandees, generals, leading statesmen, famous scholars and fellow-poets were all represented. Hardly a single famous name of the period, except that of the Emperor Ch'ien Lung himself, is missing. Partly in order to escape from personal congratulations at Nanking he arranged for the marriage of his son Yuan Ch'ih to take place on his birthday and went with him to fetch the bride from Ningpo. She was the daughter of his old friend Shen Jung-ch'ang, a member of one of the foremost Ningpo families, but himself rather unsuccessful in his public career. The girl, Ch'üan-pao ('Complete treasure'), had learnt, from a cousin who lived in the house, how to write poetry, which Yuan's son had never been able to do. 'It looks', writes Yuan Mei, 'as though the family art of poetry will have to descend in the female line.' Near Ningpo he visited the shrine of his 'fifth generation ancestor' Yuan Huai-pin and saw there tablets recording his own election to the Han-lin Academy and his brother Yuan Shu's success in taking the Third Degree. These had presumably been sent by the family, but Yuan Mei himself had never been there before. At Ningpo too he visited the T'ien-i Ko, the most famous private library in Chinese history, founded by Fan Ch'in (1506–1585) in the middle of the sixteenth century. In 1773 the head of the family had sent all the rarer books to Peking, to be copied in connection with Ch'ien Lung's great Imperial Library scheme. It is evident that, contrary to what some accounts suggest, the originals had not been returned to their owner at the time of Yuan's visit. 'The cases are there, but the jewels have departed', he writes, with the note: 'The Sung dynasty printed books and the rare manuscripts that were in the boxes have all disappeared.' Another member of the Fan family, however, still had a collection of about a thousand letters, dating from the Ming dynasty. 'Here', he writes, 'I had better luck, and was even allowed to scribble two or three lines in the margin of one of the letters.' The letter in question was one by Yang Ssu-ch'ang, who in 1641 starved himself to death, after failing to defeat the rebel Chang Hsien-chung.

His travels this spring (1795) were greatly aided by the kindness of Ch'i-feng-e (1746–1806), who lent him a comfortable boat and put several of his own servants at his disposal. 'In all the eighty years of my life', he says in his letter of thanks, 'I have never been the recipient of such limitless generosity and kindness.' Ch'i-feng-e was an 'honorary Manchu' of Korean origin. In 1796 he got into trouble for failing to investigate properly a falsification of accounts by the Imperial Textile Factory. For a while he had charge of the Yuan-ming-yuan palace near Peking, but was later banished to Turkestan.

On returning from his travels in the summer of 1795, Yuan wrote a number of poems about old age:

Now that I am old I get up very early
And feel like God creating a new world.
I come and go, meeting no one on the way;
Wherever I look, no kitchen-smoke rises.
I want to wash, but the water has not been heated;
I want to drink, but no tea has been made.
My boys and girls are behind closed doors;
My man-servants and maid-servants are all fast asleep.
At first I am cross and feel inclined to shout;
But all of a sudden remember my young days—
How I too in those early morning hours
Lay snoring, and hated to leave my bed.

I find myself going in a certain direction
And am quite sure that I had some plan in my mind.
But by the time I have got half-way
I cannot remember what I wanted to do.
Or again I call out for a servant to come
Evidently meaning to give him some instruction.
By the time he arrives I forget that I have called
And ask instead what he is doing here. . . .

If I step into the garden, a servant rushes to hold me;
If I climb the stairs, the whole household panics.
Whatever I do, someone is sorry for me;
That is what makes being old detestable!

When I was young and had no money to spend
I had a passionate longing for expensive things.
I was always envying people for their fur coats,
For the wonderful things they got to eat and drink.
I dreamt of these things, but none of them came my way,
And in the end I became very depressed.
Nowadays, I have got quite smart clothes,
But am old and ugly, and they do not suit me at all.
All the choicest foods are on my table;
But I only manage to eat a few scraps.
I feel inclined to say to my Creator
'Let me live my days on earth again,
But this time be rich when I am young;
To be poor when one is old does not matter at all.'

On the eighteenth day of the tenth month (1795) he fell ill:

If one falls ill, it does not mean one is dying;
But when one is old, anything may happen.
They have sent for a whole series of doctors and healers;
My children sat with me till the third watch.
But an old tree withstands wind and frost;
An idle cloud lightly stays or goes.
This winter cricket's wings must both be there,
Or it would not be able still to fashion its songs.

In the winter he recommended Liu Chih-p'eng to Tseng Yü (1760–1831), Transport Commissioner at Yangchow. Ts'eng was a poet and patron of literature. He seems to have got on well with Liu and to have given him a small job of some kind. Some time during 1794 Liu had 'moved to the Southern Garden'. This was an area to the south-west of Soochow where there had once been a famous garden. He may have needed a salary in order to keep the place up.

Yuan Mei had now so far recovered as to go and dine with Ch'en Feng-tzu (1726–1799), the Financial Commissioner of Nanking. The food and wine were both excellent, and he got very drunk, a thing which in his whole life had rarely happened to him. Towards the end of the year he wrote:

Everything else in life is easy to break with;
Only my books are hard to leave behind.
I want to go through them all again,
But the days hurry by, and there is not time.
If I start on the Classics I shall never get to history;
If I read philosophy, literature goes by the board.
I look back at the time when I purchased them—
Thousands of dollars, I never worried about the price.
If passages were missing, the pains I took to supply them,
And to fill out sets that were incomplete!
Of the finest texts many are copied by hand;
The toil of which fell to my office clerks.
Day and night I lived with them in intimacy.
I numbered their volumes and marked them with yellow and red.
How many branches of wax-candle light,
How many drops of weary heart's blood!
My sons and grandsons know nothing of this;
Perhaps the book-worms could tell their own tale.
Today I have had a great tidy-up,
And feel I have done everything I was born to do. . . .
It is good to know that the people in the books
Are waiting lined up in the Land of the Dead.
In a little while I shall meet them face to face
And never again need to look at what they wrote!

In 1796 came a horrified letter from an old friend called Chu Kuei (1731–1806) saying that he had come across an edition of Yuan's later poems in which his companion on the 1782–1786 excursions was mentioned by 'name and surname'.

'I picked up a writing brush', says Chu Kuei, 'and crossed out the name, thinking I should ill requite your friendship for me if I did not take steps to cover up your offence.' 'Is it an offence to make excursions?', asked Yuan Mei in his reply. 'Or if the offence consisted in a teacher going with a pupil, what about the excursion to the Rain Altars that Confucius made with his disciple Fan Ch'ih? Or if it is wrong for an old man to go about with young ones, how was it that Confucius went jaunting not with staid contemporaries, but with "newly-capped youths"? Or is it that you have some personal objection to Liu? You live six thousand leagues away. You have never seen him or heard him speak, you do not even know where he lives or what he does, and yet you have so violent a feeling against him that you take up your brush and cross out his name. . . . If people hear of it, they will be bound to think that Liu has committed some enormity so frightful that no right-minded gentleman could allow his name to remain on the pages of my book. What do you take him for? Let me tell you that he is a descendant of the great Liu Tsung-chou, behaves in an exemplary way to his parents and friends, and is an accomplished writer both of prose and verse. It is true that he is good-looking, and it may have been a great mistake on his part not to have arranged with the Maker of Things, at the time of his birth, to give him an ugly face. By not doing so he no doubt brought upon himself a lot of subsequent criticism. But it appears that such things lie in the hands of the goddess Nü Kua, who moulds her clay as she pleases, and Liu's wishes were not consulted. I have five or six other disciples at the Sui-yuan who happen also to be very good-looking. If they hear of this they will all be wondering whether they too are not in danger.'

Chu Kuei was President of the Board of War and, during part of this year (1796), was Governor-General of Kwantung and Kwangsi, with his headquarters at Canton. It was no doubt here that he heard accounts of Liu's goings-on there in 1784; for example, the episode with Prefect Wu's door-keeper (see above p. 155).

This year Yuan Mei was away at Yangchow and Soochow most of the time. He was finding strangely enough that in his old age his sight had improved, and that he no longer needed his spectacles:

Who is it that, now I am old, has given me new eyes?
I have lately stopped wearing my goggles, and see better than before.
You and I have grown old together; you have stood me in good stead,
'Lending me light' for thirty years. But now it is time to part.
Just as my spring is drawing to its close the ice at last has melted;
Almost at dawn the moon of my days has suddenly doubled its light.
From now onward the bridge of my nose and my ears on each side
Will be free from your irksome tugging and dangling for all the rest of my days.

He suffered at this time from sleeplessness:

Since I grew old and my soul decayed, all night I cannot sleep,
While mark by mark the float sinks till it touches the Fifth Watch.
Oh that someone would take me by the hand and lead me to the Land of Sleep;
Gladly would I give a year of life as barter for a single dream!

The 'float' of course refers to the water-clock. Another poem of this period refers to the belief that the 'widower-fish' (a kind of pike) cannot close its eyes:

Now that I am old I am frightened of the night, for it seems longer than a year;
I might as well be a widower-fish, so little do I sleep.
I watch as eagerly for day as a candidate watches for the lists;
Not till the first salvo of dawn does my torment draw to its close.

But he was still very active. He records that in this year (1796) he acquired five lady pupils, and towards the close of the year he was finishing his Cookery Book (*Shih Tan*, 'The Menu'): 'in the intervals of writing poetry I compose my Cookery Book'. It seems, however, that the Cookery Book, perhaps in an incomplete form, had been circulating in manuscript for some years before this. For many years past he had been in the habit, whenever he particularly enjoyed a dish at a friend's house, of sending round his cook to take a lesson in making this dish. The composing of the cookery book consisted largely in arranging these recipes in systematic order, and writing a few pages of general introduction. In his exhortations and warnings, at the beginning, he is evidently hard put to it to think of anything to say. One does not need a major poet to tell one that the cook must keep his hands clean and not let ashes fall into the food, or that the ingredients must be fresh and in good condition. One is reminded, in reading him, of the B.B.C. auntie who tells us that bacon tastes nicer when it is not green.

Westerners who have heard of Yuan Mei generally associate his name with the cookery book, owing to the fact that Professor Giles translated some passages from it in his *History of Chinese Literature* and elsewhere. It was also translated into French by a writer using the pseudonym Panking, in 1924. Here are a few extracts from it:

> A good cook cannot with the utmost application produce more than four successful dishes in one day, and even then it is hard for him to give proper attention to every detail; and he certainly won't get through unless everything is in its right place and he is on his feet the whole time. It is no use to give him a lot of assistants; each of them will have his own ideas, and there will be no proper discipline. The more help he gets, the worse the results will be. I once dined with a merchant. There were three successive sets of dishes and sixteen different sweets. Altogether, more than forty kinds of food were served. My host regarded the

dinner as an enormous success. But when I got home I was so hungry that I ordered a bowl of plain rice-gruel. From this it may be imagined how little there was, despite this profusion of dishes, that was at all fit to eat.

I always say that chicken, pork, fish and duck are the original geniuses of the board, each with a flavour of its own, each with its distinctive style; whereas sea-slug and swallows-nest (despite their costliness) are commonplace fellows, with no character—in fact, mere hangers-on. I was once asked to a party given by a certain Governor, who gave us plain boiled swallows-nest, served in enormous vases, like flower-pots. It had no taste at all. The other guests were obsequious in their praise of it. But I said: 'We are here to eat swallows-nest, not to take delivery of it wholesale.' If our host's object was simply to impress, it would have been better to put a hundred pearls into each bowl. Then we should have known that the meal had cost him tens of thousands, without the unpleasantness of being expected to eat what was uneatable.

When I was at Peking there was a certain gentleman who was very fond of inviting guests, but the food was not at all good. One day a guest said to him, 'Do you count me as a good friend?' 'Certainly I do', said the host. The guest then knelt in front of him, saying, 'If you are indeed my friend, I have a request to make to you, and I shall not rise from my knees till it is granted'. 'What is your request?', asked the astonished host. 'That you will promise', said the guest, 'that in future when you ask people to dinner, you will not ask me.'

Governor Yang's Western Ocean (i.e. *European*) *Wafer*.

Take the white of an egg and some flour-powder and mix them into a paste. Make a pair of metal shears with at their ends two plates the shape of the wafer, about the size of a small dish. There should be less than a tenth of an inch between the two surfaces when the scissors close. Heat on a fierce fire. All that is needed is your paste, your scissors and the fire. In a moment the wafer will be finished, white as snow and lustrous as glazed paper. On top, add a powdering of frosted sugar and pine-kernels.

In the year *ping-hsu* (1766) I stayed at Li-shui with Mr. Yeh, and he gave me 'black groats' (*wu-fan*) wine to drink. When I had consumed sixteen cups those present began to be rather concerned, and advised me to stop. I was already reeling, but could not bring myself to keep my hands off it.

It is black in colour; the taste very sweet and fresh. But its excellence is really beyond anything that can be put into words. I was told that at Li-shui when a girl is born they always make a jar of this wine, using high quality dark cooked-millet. They do not open it till the girl's wedding day, so that it is drunk at the earliest fifteen or sixteen years after it is made. When the jar is opened, half has evaporated. What remains is so thick that it is like glue in the mouth and its perfume is so strong that it can be smelt even outside the room.

(By the late summer of 1797 the cookery book had already been printed.)

Early in 1797 he had a bad relapse which he attributed to having been given *shen-ch'i* (apparently a kind of ginseng). After a month a friend recommended sulphur. Yuan's family were aghast, as sulphur was considered to be a very violent and dangerous drug. But three doses of it completely undid the evil effects of the *shen-ch'i*. Another friend wrote urging him to give up taking medicines altogether.

In his weak state he found that reading his own poems was the employment that suited him best:

What is the thing best suited for someone who is lying ill?
To open a book is about as much as I have strength to do.

To delight my ears I may casually listen to a bird outside the window,
But for pleasure of the mind I nowadays read only my own poems.
The far-off doings of all my life lie there, one upon another;
Ten thousand leagues, from place to place, I follow my journey's course.
I have read through six thousand three hundred poems;
It is almost as though those spring dreams were mine to live again.

The Chinese believe, as we do, that to be born under the planet Jove gives one a laughing, 'jovial' nature. One of Yuan Mei's disciples (Li Hsien-ch'iao) even suggests that Yuan was the Spirit of the Planet Jupiter, lodging for a while on earth as a 'hero of the comic'. His laughter still resounded through the house in the days of his last illness:

The east wind again has brought the splendour of spring flowers;
The willows gradually turn more green, the grass gradually sprouts.
When I look into the stream I must not repine at the snow on my two brows;
How few people have lived to see the flowers of four reigns!
Every moment I am now given comes as a gift from Heaven;
There is no limit to the glorious things that happen in the spring.
If you want to call, you need only pause outside the hedge and listen;
The place from which most laughter comes is certain to be my house!

But he was not always in the mood for laughing:

The first sign of farewell to life
Is the turning inside out of all one's tastes.

The great drinker stops caring for wine,
The traveller wants only to be left where he is.
My life-long passion was my love of company,
And the more my visitors talked, the better I liked them.
But ever since my illness came upon me
At the first word I at once stop up my ears.
And worse still, when my wife or children come
I cannot bring myself even to wave a hand.
I know that this is a very bad sign;
My old body has almost done its task.
But strangely enough I go through my old books
With as great delight as I did in former days.
And ill though I am I still write poems,
Chanting them aloud till the night is far spent.
Shall it be 'push the door' or 'knock at the door'?
I weigh each word, each line from beginning to end.
I see to it that every phrase is alive;
I do not accept a single dead word.
Perhaps the fact that this habit has not left me
Shows that I still have a little longer to live.

The 'push' *versus* 'knock' is an allusion, and a very apt one, to the ninth-century poet Chia Tao who was encountered in the streets of the Capital 'pushing' and 'knocking' in the air with his hands, in an effort to decide which word he ought to use in a poem he was composing.

It was a cold summer:

There is no mistaking that the surface of the pond is covered with lotus leaves;
Mid-summer has just been feted, yet the air has an autumn chill.
Heaven, deciding that an old invalid should look like an old invalid
Is forcing him in the sixth month still to be wrapped in furs.

A letter came from Liu Chih-p'eng enclosing a medical prescription and asking for details about Yuan Mei's health.

This is the last we hear of him; he was now no longer a dashing young man-about-town, but a middle-aged minor official (perhaps about 37 at this time), and judging from the poems by him that Yuan Mei includes in his collection of poems by friends, much sobered down.

This year there was an 'intercalary' sixth month—an extra month put in, as I have already explained, to keep the solar and lunar years in step. On the fifteenth of this extra month Yuan Mei drew up the document that is generally called his Will. It contains, in fact, instructions for the immediate transference of most of his property, during his lifetime, to his nephew and son; and also further instructions that were to take effect when he died. He gives a general account of his career in order to explain how it is that, having started with nothing, he is now able to leave to his heirs no less than thirty thousand ounces of silver (about £10,000 at the then current rate of exchange), 'a sum far beyond what in early days I ever expected, and sufficient to keep both of you in comfort'. Then after speaking of his pictures, curios and so on he says:

> 'I want you two to keep them properly dusted and cleaned and put back in their proper cupboards, so that when people call they may see them looking just as they did in my lifetime. If that can be kept up for thirty years, I shall rest contented in my grave. Of any longer period it is useless to think. What may have happened by that time neither you nor I can know.' Actually the house and its treasures remained virtually intact till 1853, when the whole area was laid waste by the T'ai-p'ing revolutionaries. After directions about the care of family graves, he goes on: 'My prose works, works in parallelistic style (*wai-chi*), poems, letters, poetry talks and essays on the classics, the poems by my three sisters, the collection of poems by friends, the ghost stories and cookery-book—of all these the blocks are here and you must take care of them and jointly arrange for their printing and sale.

'As regards notices of my death, you are to manage them between you. I would rather you sent out too few than too many. Those intended for people of high rank or position should be on light pink paper and the announcement should be in small letters. Uncoloured paper must not be used. For distribution to ordinary people, small, antique slips are the really refined thing. The sending out of large sheets of paper is a vulgarity.

'At Nanking it has become customary for placards to be published, just like those by which pedlars announce their wares, inviting all men of substance and position to attend at the ritual lamentations. This is a bad custom, and I hereby forbid you to do anything of the kind. It will be quite enough if three or four people with whom I was on intimate terms get together and mourn for a couple of days. There is no need to compose an account of my life for this occasion; for there already exists Academician Wu's notice, a copy of which should be given to each of the mourners. . . . You can see what is to be spent on my burial by referring to the bills for your grandparent's interment. You are to share the expenses, which should not come to more than fifty ounces of silver. I should not like more to be spent than I spent on my parents. The only monument (on the path to the tomb) is to be a slab bearing the inscription:

> "Tomb of Yuan, of the Sui-yuan, Ch'ing dynasty. For a thousand autumns and ten thousand generations there will certainly be those who appreciate me."'

It should here be mentioned that the inscription on the tomb itself was a short factual account of his life written by his friend Yao Nai. The Will continues:

'There is something I particularly want to enjoin upon you both. A-t'ung (his nephew and heir) is apt to be impatient. With him it is a case of tiger's head and snake's tail; he begins things, but leaves them unfinished. A-ch'ih (his own son) is apt to be timid, and this makes him stand-offish and cold. It is best that they should both realize their shortcomings, against the time when there is no one to help them. . . .

'As for recitation of Scriptures, chanting of liturgies and entertainment of monks on the seventh days—these are things that I have always detested. You may tell your sisters to come and make an offering to me, in which case I shall certainly accept it; or to come once and wail; at which I shall be deeply moved. But if monks come to the door, at the first sound of their wooden clappers, my divine soul will stop up its ears and run away, which I am sure you would not like.'

In a codicil, after some further directions about the disposition of his main property, he says:

'If there is any money left over, I wish it to be used in giving mementos to my daughters and their sons and nephews and, outside the family, to long-standing disciples, trusted servants, to the local beadle and his assistants. . . . As I have said, all my works have already been printed. The only exception is the *Sui Pi* (scholastic jottings) in 30 chapters. I was thinking of getting it printed when my great sickness suddenly came, and I did no more about it. I hope that one day you two, when you have nothing better to do, will arrange together to get it printed, and then fix a price for it and publish it. By doing so you ought to make some profit.'

After drawing up this document he went to Yangchow to see a doctor. The new treatment seemed at first to be a great success:

I know that my old wife must be worrying about me
And hastily scribble a few lines of news.
Wanting to please her, I cannot resist the temptation
To make things out even better than they are. . . .

The improvement lasted till the twentieth of the ninth month:

The same illness has been with me for over a year;
It has shifted its ground, but I did not weed it out.
Like a bird in the air, I have risen to sink again;
Like the fish in the pool, I come only to go.
I seem to be in port, only to find myself at sea;
The chariot moves, but at once the steeds are unyoked.
'God's children' indeed! It is He who is the child,
And we mortals the toys with which He plays.

He died on the seventeenth of the eleventh month; January 3, 1798, according to the Western calendar.

The account I have given of Yuan Mei consists so largely of quotations from his works, both in prose and verse, as almost to be an anthology. It is certainly far from being what is called a 'critical biography'. Still less is it a Life and Times; and indeed he was, during all but a few years in his career, so completely sequestered from the political events of the day that it would be profitless to discuss him in connection with them. The only aspect of Manchu policy that touched him closely was the Literary Inquisition, and to this I have paid a good deal of attention. In many ways his outlook was typical of his time. His anti-puritanism, his scepticism about many supposedly ancient texts, his dislike of Neo-Confucian metaphysics, his view that women had a right to be educated, were attitudes that were characteristic of the period. Even the ultra-conservative Shen Te-ch'ien, who disagreed with so many of Yuan Mei's opinions, appears to have shared his view about female education; for he too accepted lady-pupils. The one respect (apart from his genius as a writer) in which Yuan Mei seems to have been unique was his persistence, despite the advice of many friends, in publishing writings of a sort that other authors suppressed. It was thought clownish and undignified to print humorous poems, and improper to print references to concubines, young actors, and so on. But in Yuan Mei's view it is the highest duty of a poet to preserve the truth (*ts'un ch'i chen*) to show all things, himself included, as they really are. Added to this was a sense of loyalty to those whom he loved. Why hush up the fact that Liu, whose society had added so greatly to his happiness, went with him on his travels, merely because the world regarded Liu as a disreputable character? Would it have been human, I think he felt, to write epitaphs about a host of indifferent acquaintances, and none, for example, about Miss Fang, the concubine who served him devotedly for twenty-four years? Yet for writings of this kind he was bitterly criticized. But other reasons were at work. To have hushed up certain aspects of his life might have seemed to imply that he was ashamed of them; and he was not. He lived in strict accord with principles which, though like other philosophies they may have been adopted to justify his behaviour, seemed to him valid and respectable. Finally, there was undoubtedly a streak of impishness, even of impudence in him, which made him enjoy shocking people.

When one turns to the question of his art as a writer and its actual value, I find the subject a very difficult one. In my view the value of literature depends neither on content nor on form, but on the relation between the two. To discuss this relation I must obviously be able to quote in the original, which is not here possible. To deal with the relation between Yuan's content and a translated form would be quite irrelevant.

Despite their imperfections my translations have in the past done something towards inspiring a number of people with the idea that, for lovers of poetry, Chinese is a language worth learning. I hope that this book may serve the same purpose and in particular do something to dispel the common idea that all good Chinese poetry belongs to a remote antiquity.

APPENDIX I

Anson's dealings with the Chinese at Canton

Yuan Mei's account of Commodore Anson's dealings with the Chinese at Canton in 1743.

(Prose VIII.4)

IN 1743, H.M.S. *Centurion*, commanded by Commodore Anson, after capturing a Spanish galleon of vastly superior size, towed her to the mouth of the Canton River. Here Anson attempted to purchase supplies and refit his ship. But for weeks on end the Chinese authorities obstructed him in every possible way. Anson assumed that they had written to Peking asking for instructions, and were fobbing him off till they received a reply. In the end, however (so the English believed), the Chinese were so much impressed by the courage and efficiency displayed by Anson and some of his sailors in helping to put out a fire at Canton, that they suddenly decided to let him buy provisions, refit and set out unmolested for England, Anson having first handed over to the Chinese (who were neutral in the Anglo-Spanish war) several hundred Spanish prisoners, with a view to their being returned to the Philippines. Yuan Mei's account is as follows: 'In the eighth year of Ch'ien Lung (1743) the Red Haired Country (i.e. the English) attacked Luzon and conquered it, capturing about five hundred men, with whom they sailed to the mouth of the Canton River. There was great alarm in Canton and the Governor-General, sending for the Provincial Treasurer T'o-yung, said to him, "When outside barbarians who are at war with one another conduct their hostilities on our very borders, ought we to allow it or ought we to annihilate them? Which course would best further our national interests?" "What we should do", said T'o-yung, "is to make them hand over their five hundred prisoners under the specific title of Tribute and request Your Excellency to deal with them as he thinks fit." The Governor-General smiled ruefully. "You can only be joking", he said. "The Red Haired People are barbarians, but they are not fools. How can you suppose that, returning as complete victors after their enormous voyage, they will now submit to being ordered about? You advise this course, but would you yourself be able to carry it out?" "If I were not sure that it is possible", said T'o-yung, "I would not have dared to suggest it." "If you know how it can be done", said the Governor-General, looking more unconvinced than ever, "tell me what resources you will need." "Very little", said T'o-yung. "All I ask is that you should put Prefect Yin and Colonel Yang under my orders, and in six days I will come back and report. The Prefect is extremely gifted and intelligent; the Colonel, with his imposing figure and great beard, looks the typical man of war." The Governor-General consented and T'o-yung, sending for the Prefect, said to him, "You are to go to the Red Haired people and tell them to send in a Memorial, undertaking to hand over their five hundred prisoners to the Governor-General, under the specific title of Tribute, for His Excellency to deal with as he thinks fit." The Prefect was as much astonished as the Governor-General had been, and at first raised some objection. "Reflect a little", answered T'o-yung. "These Red Haired people had to cross several thousand leagues of ocean in order to attack Luzon. It is certain that they are short of provisions, and as they have encountered heavy storms, it is equally certain that their ship must need repairs, without which they cannot embark on the homeward voyage. . . . " The Prefect was completely won over and went with Colonel Yang, who had with him five men in uniform and armed with cross-bows, to the Lion Wharf (at the mouth of the Canton River) where the Colonel and his men bivouacked, while the Prefect went to the provision merchants' shops and privately instructed them to withhold all supplies. When the Red Haired people came to see what was afoot the Prefect said to them: "We Chinese are afraid that rogues may be tempting you to waste your money on things you do not really need, and we are here to protect you." The Red Haired people went away rather puzzled. It was soon observed that less and less smoke was rising from their cook-house, and before long their Commander (i.e. Commodore Anson) came and asked if he might speak to the Prefect. When he was seated, but before he had time to say anything, Prefect Yin began to revile him, saying, "For long past it has been a strict rule with us that the Bogue was to be regarded as the frontier of China. But now, being at war with another country, instead of quickly passing the Bogue with furled ensigns, you flaunt your arms there. This is open rebellion. Our Governor-General is a man of violent disposition and delights in warfare. We were therefore reluctant to tell him of your misdeeds and preferred instead to set up a guard here, in order to starve you to death first, and afterwards to inform the Governor-General." Upon this, the Commander of the Red Haired people fell into complete despair. He glanced at the Colonel; but the Colonel, signalling to him to be silent, his hair and beard bristling with rage, poured out upon him the most ferocious curses. More frightened than ever the foreign Commander flung himself upon the ground, saying: "It is true indeed that we are at the end of our resources. But we had no intention of offending your Heavenly Court, and I implore you to forgive us and tell us what we should do." At this the Prefect indicated that it would make a difference if the prisoners were presented as tribute. "If matters could be settled on these terms", said the foreigner, weeping, "I would indeed account it a Heavenly blessing. I beg of you to tell the Governor-General that I accept." "I cannot do that", said the Prefect. "All I can do is to inform the Provincial Treasurer, and he might then pass on what you have said to the Governor-General. But these messages would have to pass through various other channels, often difficult of access. Moreover, if when it comes to the point you fail to carry out your side of the bargain, it will be we who will get into trouble. No! I dare not do it." "How would it be if I, the Red Haired one, were myself to present a memorial to His Excellency, asking for provisions on these terms?" When the foreigner said this, the Prefect, pretending to make the concession with the utmost reluctance, told him he might try this. The upshot was that the foreigner, with his cross-bow under his arm, his arrow-case on his back and his hands touching his forehead, crept on his knees into the presence of the Governor-General and presented a memorial in which he offered his five hundred prisoners as tribute, begging His Excellency to dispose of them as he deemed best. The Governor-General was delighted, returned the prisoners to Luzon, gave presents to the Red Hairs and allowed them to sail home to their country.'

Anson's account, as sent to the Admiralty (*London Gazette*, June 16) was as follows: 'The Vice-king received me with great civility and politeness, and granted me everything I desired'!

Yuan Mei's story is of course not to be taken as sober history. It is an anecdote (strongly resembling a scene from Chinese drama) intended to illustrate the resourcefulness and sagacity of T'o-yung, and embellished by Yuan with touches of his own, such as Anson's improbable bow and arrows. But it serves to correct two wrong impressions given by the English accounts. There is no evidence that Governor-General Tsereng made any report to Peking about the episode until after Anson's departure. He held up Anson at Canton not, as the English thought, because he was waiting for instructions from Peking, but in order to bring pressure to bear on Anson to hand over his prisoners as Tribute. Secondly, he let Anson go not because of the gallantry of the Commodore and his men in putting out the fire, but because Anson had undertaken to hand over his prisoners.

Anson was, of course, not aware that by handing over prisoners 'as Tribute' he was admitting the suzeraignty of China over Great Britain. This, from the Chinese point of view, was most definitely so. Apart from ancient historical examples, the word Tribute (*kung*) implies this; for it means what an inferior offers to a superior. The Governor-General assumed that Anson knew the symbolic significance of handing over prisoners-of-war and that he would not be willing to part with them except under the strongest possible pressure. But in reality 'Mr. Anson was extremely desirous to get rid of the Spaniards, who were a great incumbrance to him.' It was a typical game of diplomatic blind man's buff.

The value of Yuan Mei's account is that it brings out the importance, in Chinese eyes, of the handing over of the Spanish prisoners. This the English accounts quite fail to do. But though there are at least four English accounts, the only at all extensive one is that of Richard Walter (*Voyage Round the World*, *1748*). This has the disadvantage that Walter left the *Centurion* and returned to England before the episode in question, and we do not know where his information about subsequent happenings comes from.

Prefect Yin, who figures so importantly in the story, was Yin Kuang-jen, at that time prefect of Tungkwan, near Canton. He is well known both as an official and a writer. We owe to him the standard account of the Portugese settlement at Macao (*Ao-men Chi Lueh*). This contains a brief reference to the Anson episode and is the only source that gives the Chinese version of his name—An-hsin. In about 1790, when Prefect Yin died, Yuan Mei wrote a sketch of his life in which the Anson episode is again briefly alluded to, and we are told that after the prisoners had been sent back to the Philippines, an account of the whole affair was sent to the Emperor, who entirely approved of the way in which the Governor-General had handled it.

APPENDIX II

After Yuan Mei's Death

'AFTER his death there were very bitter attacks upon him, more than half of them made by disciples and old friends. When the news of his death reached Yangchow, Wu Tzu (1755–1821) and I were the only people to join together and perform the ritual lamentations for him.'

So says Wu Sung-liang, the young poet whom Yuan Mei got to know in 1793 (see above p. 184) and whom he so much admired, in his *Poetry Talks*, quoted in the *Kuo-ch'ao Ch'i-hsien Lei-cheng* Ch. 234, f. 23. Who these 'disciples and old friends' were Wu does not say. The only attacks that I know of were those of the philosopher of history Chang Hsueh-ch'eng who (see above p. 101) regarded Yuan Mei as a perverter of youth and in particular disapproved of his accepting women as pupils. But the onslaughts were made shortly before Yuan's death, not after it. And how, one wonders, did Wu ascertain that in the huge city of Yangchow, no other mourning-parties were formed? In any case, we know from Yuan Mei's Will that he wished to be formally mourned for only by a few close friends.

It is clear that in Yuan Mei's life-time he was generally regarded as the foremost literary man of the age. The usual view of him later on, as expressed in books of reference and in standard histories of Chinese literature, is that though some of his poetry lacks seriousness and dignity, and is over-concerned with sensual pleasures, he is one of the two or three best poets of the Ch'ien Lung period. But such assessments are usually copied from one book to another and do not represent the considered opinion of the author. The most unfavourable view that I happen to have come across is that of Liang Ch'i-ch'ao (1869–1929) who on p. 169 of his *Ch'ing Tai Hsueh-shu* ('Scholarship in the Ch'ing dynasty'), 1927, says that the works of Yuan Mei 'smell so putrid that one cannot go near them'. If this great man, the last traditional Chinese philosopher, could have brought himself to venture a little closer, he would have found that out of Yuan Mei's many thousand poems and other works, not more than a mere handful could possibly be objected to on moral grounds. Here again Liang may merely be repeating a view expressed by someone else.

APPENDIX III

The Macartney Mission and Yuan Mei's Works

THE only member of the Mission who knew any Chinese was G. T. Staunton, aged twelve, who accompanied the Ambassador as page. According to the Dictionary of National Biography he presented '3,000 Chinese volumes' to the Royal Asiatic Society. It occurred to me that it might have been he who acquired Yuan Mei's Works in 1793 and that the book might be among those that he presented to the Society. It turns out, however, that 'volumes' means chapters (*chüan*) not separate books. Staunton presented only about 250 separate works, and among them there is nothing by Yuan Mei. The Society possesses Yuan Mei's Ghost Stories and his Letters in editions that are early, but subsequent to 1793. I am indebted to Miss Fell the librarian for information on this point.

APPENDIX IV

Rules Observed

1. *In giving dates I have followed the common practice of calling, for example, 1797 the year which corresponds* en gros *with the Western 1797.*
2. *Whenever possible I have referred to people by their official name* (ming).
3. *In order to limit the number of persons mentioned I have* (a) *said very little about Yuan's relatives;* (b) *not mentioned a number of friends about whom little is known; for example Yin-chi-shan's numerous sons.*
4. *I have omitted the purely conventional dirges on the death of friends.*
5. *I have not mentioned minor excursions (for example, to Hangchow and Yangchow) unless there was a special reason for doing so.*
6. *To have used Chinese characters would have increased the cost of the book for the benefit of a small proportion of readers. The characters for almost all the ancient persons will be found in Giles's* Biographical Dictionary, *and those for Manchu dynasty names in Hummel's* Eminent Chinese of the Ch'ing Period.
7. *I have followed the common practice of writing 'the Emperor Ch'ien Lung' rather than 'the Ch'ien Lung Emperor'.*
8. *I have rendered official titles in a loose way, merely trying to indicate the sort of position referred to. Thus I have used 'Governor' as the translation of several different terms.*
9. *I have followed the Wade system of transcription, but left out some diacritic signs.*

Books

1. Sources

My main source has been Yuan Mei's Complete Works (*Sui-yuan Ch'üan Chi*) in sixty-four fascicules, bearing the date 1918 and published by the Wen-ming Shu-chü, Shanghai. A list of books containing biographical notices of Ch'ing dynasty persons will be found in *Index to Thirty-three Collections of Ch'ing Dynasty Biographies* (Harvard-Yenching Institute, 1932); I have made extensive use of Nos. 1, 2 and 3, and also of the *Shih Lu* (Court Records) of the period. I am deeply indebted to *Eminent Chinese of the Ch'ing Period*, edited by A. W. Hummel (1944), and to Professor L. C. Goodrich's excellent book *The Literary Inquisition of Ch'ien-lung* (1935).

2. Previous studies of Yuan Mei

C. Imbault-Huart's article 'Un Poète Chinois du XVIIIe Siècle' (*Journal of the North China Branch, Royal Asiatic Society*, Vol. XIX, 1884) was a notable piece of pioneering, but is based on a knowledge of only certain parts of Yuan's works. Yang Hung-lieh's *Yuan Mei as a Great Thinker* (1927) remains, so far as I know, the best study of Yuan in Chinese; though its main thesis—that Yuan Mei was important as a philosopher and scholar—seems to me untenable.

References

(In the case of Yuan Mei's own poems references have generally not been given, as they are arranged chronologically and are easy to find. For the edition of Yuan's Works used, see above, p. 214.)

p. 11 Aunt Shen, Prose V. 5.
p. 12 introduction to poetry, Shih Hua VI. 8b.
p. 13 no money to buy books, Poems XXXII. 3b.
p. 13 Essay on Kuo Chü, Prose XX. 8.
p. 14 'National horse', Shih Hua XII. 6b.
p. 15 Poem on Spring Snow, Shih Hua XIV. 4b.
p. 15 'came out in vanguard', Shih Hua XII. 2.
p. 15 Mr. Ch'ai, Shih Hua XII. 7.
p. 15 Sufferings on boat, see Will (*Works*, fasc. 1).
p. 16 Uncle, Shih Hua II. 10b.
p. 18 Uncle's greeting, see Will.
p. 19 The Golden Pheasant, Shih Hua V. 11b.
p. 20 T'ang Shou-tsu, Prose III. 8b.
p. 21 Secretary Chao, Prose XIV. 7.
p. 24 Jade Bridle-bells, Shih Hua I. 2b.
p. 26 Ortai on candidates, Prose VIII. 1.
p. 26 Chiang Ho-ning, Prose XXXI. 4.
p. 27 Hsu Yun-t'ing, Shih Hua IV. 6b.
p. 27 Wife's age, see *Works*, fasc. 51, III. 2b.
p. 28 'Manchus more cultivated', Shih Hua Suppl. VII. 4b.
p. 28 Shih I-chih, Prose III. 4.
p. 29 Tsou and the cat, Shih Hua X. 7b.
p. 29 Ch'iu Yueh-hsiu, Poems II. 2b.
p. 31 Te-p'ei, Prose II. 6b.
p. 32 Kögler, Fu-jen Hsueh Chih III. 2 (1932).
p. 32 Poem to Te-p'ei, Poems XV. 7.

p. 32 Poem about father, Poems XVII. 9.
p. 36 Su-wen, Prose VII. 4, and XIV. 3.
p. 38 Chuang Heng-yang, Prose VII. 5.
p. 39 Gets post at Nanking through Yin-chi-shan, Poems V. 6b.
p. 40 'At the fire he met. . . . ' Shih Hua IV. 9b.
p. 41 'Do not quote the ditties. . . . ' Poems XXXVI. 5b.
p. 42 The Typhoon, Shih Hua, IV. 8a.
p. 43 Lü Wen-kuang, Prose XIV. 7.
p. 45 Post at Kao-yu, Wai Chi V. 2b., Poems V. 7a and VI. 5a.
p. 45 Soochow beauties, Wai Chi VI. 15.
p. 46 Inspecting concubine, Shih Hua XI. 9b.
p. 46 T'ao Shih-huang, Shih Hua VI. 3b. Letter to, Prose XVI. 14.
p. 49 Hsueh I-p'iao, Shih Hua V. 2a., Prose XIV. 3.
p. 50 Illness of Chiang Pao-ch'en, Tzu Pu Yü II. 7a.
p. 52 Cook, Prose VII. 9.
p. 55 Letter to Huang T'ing-kuei, Prose XVI. 2.
p. 58 Liu-pao, Prose XXXIII. 6.
p. 65 European books, Shih Lu 444, 27b.
p. 66 Chi Yun's precautions, Yueh Wei Ts'ao T'ang Pi Chi, 17. 17.
p. 66 Wine-party, Poems IX. 1.
p. 70 Dwarf, Prose VII. 12.
p. 72 Chiang Shih-ch'üan, Poems XIV. 1b.
p. 74 Play Tales (*Ch'ü Hua*), Han-hai Ts'ung-shu 106 (Part XV).
p. 77 Mock deposition, Liang-pan Ch'iu-yü-an Sui Pi by Liang Shao-jen. I. 4.
p. 78 Ch'eng T'ing-tso. See Hu Shih in Kuo-hsueh Chi K'an V. 3. 1–40.
p. 80 Letter to Ch'eng, Letters I. 5b.
p. 80 Letter to Hsiang Yung, Letters VII. 3b.
p. 81 P'eng Shao-sheng, Prose XIX. 15 and Shih Hua XIV. 13.
p. 81 P'eng's autobiography, I-hsing Chu Chi V. 6b.
p. 83 Sensations during illness, Tzu Pu Yü XVII. 3b.
p. 83 Chao Ning-ching, Shih Hua II. 1a.
p. 84 Brother willing to take Phoenix Flute, Poems XIII. 10b.
p. 85 'If one opens a book. . . . ' Poems XIII. 5b.
p. 86 Poem to Shen Ch'üan, Poems XIII. 2.
p. 87 Shen Ch'üan in Japan; see S. Sawamura in Kokka 272.

p. 87 Li Fang-ying, Prose V. 2.
p. 90 Four Episodes, Prose VIII. 4.
p. 94 Boy's song, Yo Fu Shih Chi, 86.
p. 94 Letter to Li T'ang, Letters II. 8.
p. 94 'When we first met. . . . ' Prose XXXI. 2.
p. 95 Career of Ch'eng Chin-fang, Prose XXV. 6.
p. 98 Poem to actor, Poems XXI. 4.
p. 101 Rumours of banishment, Poems XXII. 2b, Shih Hua, Supplem. VI. 6a.
p. 101 Memorial of thanks, Wai Chi I. 4.
p. 101 Chang Hsueh-ch'eng's criticisms, Chang Shih I Shu VII. 31; also V. 26 and V. 29. Hu Shih and Nai Ming-ta, Chang Shih-chai Nien-p'u (1929), p. 129.
p. 103 Parting with Yin-chi-shan, Shih Hua III. 7b.
p. 108 Tung Shih-min's mother, Prose XXXI. 2.
p. 108 Pao Chih-tao's father, Prose XXXIV. 6.
p. 108 Cost of printing, Shih Hua, XVI. 1b.
p. 114 Misinterpretation of Great Learning, Prose XXIII. 5a.
p. 118 Mother, Prose XXVII. 8.
p. 118 Strange bird, Tzu Pu Yü XXII. 3.
p. 119 Letter to Lo P'ing, Letters V. 8b.
p. 120 Story of Mr. Yeh, Tzu Pu Yü II. 1.
p. 122 Story of Yuan Shu, Ditto XI. 2.
p. 124 The Arctic, Ditto XXI. 11.
p. 126 Mission to St. Petersburg, Revue Historique. 133 (1920), 82–89.
p. 126 Ghost Wang, Tzu Pu Yü XXII. 9.
p. 129 Grandmother's grandmother, ditto XXI. 8.
p. 130 Miss Fang's image, ditto XIX. 3b.
p. 131 Actors disapproved of, ditto IV. 9b.
p. 132 Pretentious 'control', ditto, XXI. 10b.
p. 134 Red Haired People, ditto XVI. 2b.
p. 134 The Siamese, ditto XXI. 8a.
p. 134 Sing-songs, ditto XXIII. 2b.
p. 135 Myriad Buddhas, ditto XVI. 7.
p. 136 Commentary on Heart Sūtra, Poems XXXVI. 11b.
p. 136 Frauds. Tzu Pu Yü XXIII. 7.
p. 137 King Yama, ditto Supplem. X. 1.
p. 138 The 'tiger', ditto Supplem. II. 8b.

p. 139 Li Hsiang-yun, Tzu Pu Yü III. 9, Compare Shih Hua VIII. 9b.
p. 139 Yang's letter and the reply, Letters VII. 3.
p. 139 Account of Yang, Prose XXXIV. 3.
p. 142 Chao I's joke about Liu, Shih Hua II. 6a.
p. 143 Stripy Bamboo-Village, Shih Hua XII. 13.
p. 145 Presents moustaches to monastery, T'ai-p'ing Kuang Chi 405. 14.
p. 146 Wedding-custom, Shih Hua XII. 13 and Poems XXVIII. 13.
p. 148 Mr. Yü, Shi Hua XII. 12b.
p. 149 Liu's poems. Shih Hua XIV. 8.
p. 150 T'ung Yü, Prose XXVI. 4. and XXVIII. 4; Shih Hua VI. 4b; Poems XXVIII. 20b.
p. 151 The bottomless ravine, Prose XXIX. 6b.
p. 154 Chiang Shih-ch'üan. Compare Prose XXV. 10b.
p. 155 Floods at Canton, Prose XXXI. 6.
p. 155 Liu and the door-keeper, Poems XXXI. 5.
p. 157 Title of Liu's poems, Shih Hua Supplem. VIII. 9b.
p. 158 Poetic servant, Shih Hua VI. 10.
p. 159 T'ang Ying, Shih Hua, IV. 10.
p. 166 Letter of Pi Yuan, Letters VI. 10b.
p. 171 Letters to Shen Te-ch'ien, Prose XVII. 4 seq. Compare Aoki Masaru in Seidai Bungaku Hyōronshi. But Aoki, I think, misdates the letters.
p. 172 'Someone asked me.' Shih Hua III. 12.
p. 172 Li Ch'ung-hua. Shih Hua Supplem. I. 1.
p. 173 P'u Hsien. Shih Hua Supplem. IV. 2b.
p. 173 Wu Ying-fang, ditto IV. 2b.
p. 173 Tai Yü-jang, Shih Hua, XII. 1a.
p. 174 Loves all old poets, Shih Hua, IV. 9.
p. 174 Division into T'ang and Sung, Shih Hua VI. 11.
p. 176 Pirates, Prose XXXIV. 7.
p. 177 Death of Liu's wife, Hsu T'ung-jen Chi, Poems of Thanks (Works. fasc. 48) 3b.
p. 179 Kuo Lin, Shih Hua Supplem. VII. 8.
p. 182 Friend orders Works, Shih Hua Supplem. VI. 1.
p. 183 Story of Chang P'ei, ditto V. 10.
p. 184 Wu Sung-liang's Poetry Talks, quoted in Kuo-ch'ao Ch'i-hsien-lei-cheng. 234. 23.

p. 184 Wu inattentive, Poems XXXVII. 11a.
p. 185 Chang Wen-t'ao, Letters IX. 6. Poems XXXV. 4b.
p. 186 English acquire Works. Eightieth Birthday Poems II. 3b and 11a.
p. 190 Letter to Ch'i-feng-e, Letters IX. 9.
p. 192 Chu Kuei's letter, Letters IX. 1b.
p. 192 Liu mentioned by official name, Poems XXIX. 2a.
p. 195 Five new lady pupils, Poems XXXVII. 3b.
p. 195 Cookery Book, Poems XXXVI. 15a, last line.
p. 204 Miss Fang's epitaph, Wai Chi, VI. 15.
p. 209 Account of Prefect Yin, Prose XXXIV. 8.

Index and Glossary

(In the above index, as also in the list of references, italics have been used sparingly. Entries have been made analytic only where to do so seemed likely to help the reader.)